"This series is a tremendous resource for those wanting to ? understanding of how the gospel is woven throughout Sc... pastors and scholars doing gospel business from all the Scriptures. This is a biblica... logical feast preparing God's people to apply the entire Bible to all of life with heart and mind wholly committed to Christ's priorities."

BRYAN CHAPELL, President Emeritus, Covenant Theological Seminary; Senior Pastor, Grace Presbyterian Church, Peoria, Illinois

"Mark Twain may have smiled when he wrote to a friend, 'I didn't have time to write you a short letter, so I wrote you a long letter.' But the truth of Twain's remark remains serious and universal, because well-reasoned, compact writing requires extra time and extra hard work. And this is what we have in the Crossway Bible study series *Knowing the Bible*. The skilled authors and notable editors provide the contours of each book of the Bible as well as the grand theological themes that bind them together as one Book. Here, in a 12-week format, are carefully wrought studies that will ignite the mind and the heart."

R. KENT HUGHES, Visiting Professor of Practical Theology, Westminster Theological Seminary

"*Knowing the Bible* brings together a gifted team of Bible teachers to produce a high-quality series of study guides. The coordinated focus of these materials is unique: biblical content, provocative questions, systematic theology, practical application, and the gospel story of God's grace presented all the way through Scripture."

PHILIP G. RYKEN, President, Wheaton College

"These *Knowing the Bible* volumes provide a significant and very welcome variation on the general run of inductive Bible studies. This series provides substantial instruction, as well as teaching through the very questions that are asked. *Knowing the Bible* then goes even further by showing how any given text links with the gospel, the whole Bible, and the formation of theology. I heartily endorse this orientation of individual books to the whole Bible and the gospel, and I applaud the demonstration that sound theology was not something invented later by Christians, but is right there in the pages of Scripture."

GRAEME L. GOLDSWORTHY, former lecturer, Moore Theological College; author, *According to Plan*, *Gospel and Kingdom*, *The Gospel in Revelation*, and *Gospel and Wisdom*

"What a gift to earnest, Bible-loving, Bible-searching believers! The organization and structure of the Bible study format presented through the *Knowing the Bible* series is so well conceived. Students of the Word are led to understand the content of passages through perceptive, guided questions, and they are given rich insights and application all along the way in the brief but illuminating sections that conclude each study. What potential growth in depth and breadth of understanding these studies offer! One can only pray that vast numbers of believers will discover more of God and the beauty of his Word through these rich studies."

BRUCE A. WARE, Professor of Christian Theology, The Southern Baptist Theological Seminary

KNOWING THE BIBLE

J. I. Packer, Theological Editor
Dane C. Ortlund, Series Editor
Lane T. Dennis, Executive Editor

•   •   •   •   •   •

Genesis	Psalms	Jonah, Micah, and	Ephesians
Exodus	Proverbs	Nahum	Philippians
Leviticus	Ecclesiastes	Haggai, Zechariah,	Colossians and
Numbers	Song of Solomon	and Malachi	Philemon
Deuteronomy	Isaiah	Matthew	1–2 Thessalonians
Joshua	Jeremiah	Mark	1–2 Timothy and
Judges	Lamentations,	Luke	Titus
Ruth and Esther	Habakkuk, and Zephaniah	John	Hebrews
1–2 Samuel	Ezekiel	Acts	James
1–2 Kings	Daniel	Romans	1–2 Peter and Jude
1–2 Chronicles	Hosea	1 Corinthians	1–3 John
Ezra and Nehemiah	Joel, Amos, and	2 Corinthians	Revelation
Job	Obadiah	Galatians	

•   •   •   •   •   •

J. I. PACKER was the former Board of Governors' Professor of Theology at Regent College (Vancouver, BC). Dr. Packer earned his DPhil at the University of Oxford. He is known and loved worldwide as the author of the best-selling book *Knowing God*, as well as many other titles on theology and the Christian life. He served as the General Editor of the ESV Bible and as the Theological Editor for the *ESV Study Bible*.

LANE T. DENNIS is CEO of Crossway, a not-for-profit publishing ministry. Dr. Dennis earned his PhD from Northwestern University. He is Chair of the ESV Bible Translation Oversight Committee and Executive Editor of the *ESV Study Bible*.

DANE C. ORTLUND (PhD, Wheaton College) serves as senior pastor of Naperville Presbyterian Church in Naperville, Illinois. He is an editor for the Knowing the Bible series and the Short Studies in Biblical Theology series, and is the author of several books, including *Gentle and Lowly: The Heart of Christ for Sinners and Sufferers*.

PHILIPPIANS

A 12-WEEK STUDY

Ryan Kelly

WHEATON, ILLINOIS

Trade paperback ISBN: 978-1-4335-4026-4
ePub ISBN: 978-1-4335-4029-5
PDF ISBN: 978-1-4335-4027-1
Mobipocket ISBN: 978-1-4335-4028-8

Crossway is a publishing ministry of Good News Publishers.

VP		30	29	28	27	26	25	24	23	22	21
19	18	17	16	15	14	13	12	11	10	9	8

TABLE OF CONTENTS

▲

SERIES PREFACE

KNOWING THE BIBLE, as the series title indicates, was created to help readers know and understand the meaning, the message, and the God of the Bible. Each volume in the series consists of 12 units that progressively take the reader through a clear, concise study of that book of the Bible. In this way, any given volume can fruitfully be used in a 12-week format either in group study, such as in a church-based context, or in individual study. Of course, these 12 studies could be completed in fewer or more than 12 weeks, as convenient, depending on the context in which they are used.

Each study unit gives an overview of the text at hand before digging into it with a series of questions for reflection or discussion. The unit then concludes by highlighting the gospel of grace in each passage ("Gospel Glimpses"), identifying whole-Bible themes that occur in the passage ("Whole-Bible Connections"), and pinpointing Christian doctrines that are affirmed in the passage ("Theological Soundings").

The final component to each unit is a section for reflecting on personal and practical implications from the passage at hand. The layout provides space for recording responses to the questions proposed, and we think readers need to do this to get the full benefit of the exercise. The series also includes definitions of key words. These definitions are indicated by a note number in the text and are found at the end of each chapter.

Lastly, to help understand the Bible in this deeper way, we would urge the reader to use the ESV Bible and the ESV Study Bible, which are available online at esv.org. The *Knowing the Bible* series is also available online. Additional 12-week studies covering each book of the Bible will be added as they become available.

May the Lord greatly bless your study as you seek to know him through knowing his Word.

J. I. Packer and
Lane T. Dennis

WEEK 1: OVERVIEW

▶ Getting Acquainted

Paul wrote to the Philippian church to thank them for their support and prayers, and to give updates on the welfare of Epaphroditus, Timothy, and himself (matters to which we will return below under "Date and Historical Background").

But Philippians is not just a letter of thanks and updates. Ever the teacher, Paul also writes to encourage their faith and growth. More specifically:

- to spur them on to progress in their Christian growth (2:12; 3:12–17)
- to warn of those who proclaim another gospel (3:2, 18–19)
- to reiterate the true gospel and encourage them to hold tightly to it (3:3–11)
- to encourage their unity and confront any lack of unity (2:1–4; 4:2–3)
- to call them to joy and thankfulness and peace (2:18; 3:1; 4:4–7)
- to plead with them to keep their eyes on Christ and the hope of heaven (3:2–21)

Philippians is an amazingly *practical* letter—sort of a "101" on Christian living—but it is also a deeply *doctrinal* letter. For example, in Philippians 2:5–11 we find some of the clearest and most important teaching in all of Scripture on Christ and his incarnation. And yet, the primary purpose of this section of the letter is to show Jesus as a model of humility and selfless service so that the Philippian Christians might be further unified and Christlike. So the doctrinal and practical elements are inseparable and intermingled throughout Philippians. (For further background, see the *ESV Study Bible*, pages 2275–2279 or visit esv.org.)

Placing It in the Larger Story

By the time Paul writes Philippians, the events recorded in the book of Acts have all come to pass. Of course, that means that the Messiah[1] has come—living righteously, dying sacrificially, and rising victoriously. In so doing he has ushered in a new covenant for his people (Jer. 31:31–34). He has sent his followers into the world to proclaim the gospel, to make disciples of the nations, and to plant local churches. The book of Acts records just that—30 or so years of the gospel spreading and churches forming. Thus, it is clear that the kingdom has come—it is *now*. But it is also still coming. It is both *now* and *not yet*. Christians are redeemed but must keep pressing on: standing firm in their confession, working out their salvation in Christian growth, resisting false teachers, embracing suffering and persecution, holding out the gospel of hope to the world, and committing to live out Christ's love and humility with each other in the church.

Paul wrote several biblical letters to churches and individuals (Romans–Philemon). From one angle, they all share a general purpose—to encourage and equip Christians for the *advance of the gospel* (1:12) and *progress in the faith* (1:25). But, from another angle, each letter has its own unique purpose, context, background, and emphases. One distinctive of Philippians is its emphasis on *partnership* or *sharing*. The Philippian Christians share the gospel and the gospel mission with Paul, as they do among themselves as a church. This has important and far-reaching implications (See 1:5, 7, 14–19, 27; 2:1–8, 17–18, 22, 25, 30; 3:16–17; 4:1–3, 10–16).

Key Verse

"Only let your manner of life be worthy of the gospel of Christ, so that whether I come and see you or am absent, I may hear of you that you are standing firm in one spirit, with one mind striving side by side for the faith of the gospel" (Phil. 1:27).

Date and Historical Background

Paul had a long history with the Philippian Christians, beginning with the conversion of Lydia's family, a demon-possessed girl, and the Philippian jailer (Acts 16:14–40). Paul returned to Philippi at least twice, but mutual care and communication between the apostle and the Philippian church seem to have been regular. He prayed frequently for them with much thankfulness and affection (Phil. 1:3–11). The Philippians stood with Paul, financially and otherwise, when others did not (1:7; 4:14–16). In concern for Paul's present imprisonment (1:12–19) they sent one of their best men, Epaphroditus, to bring financial support and to minister to Paul's needs (2:25).

While imprisoned in Rome, in roughly AD 62, Paul pens this letter we know as Philippians. He writes to thank the Philippian church[2] for their care for him and support of his ministry. He writes to assure them that, despite his present imprisonment, the gospel is spreading (1:12–18) and he is well cared for (4:18). He also relays that Epaphroditus, their messenger, is well after having become ill on his journey to Paul (2:26–30). Epaphroditus is now returning to the Philippians with Paul's letter. Timothy, another worthy servant and Paul's "right-hand man," may be coming in due course (2:19); and Paul himself is eager to do the same, if the Lord permits (1:8, 25–26).

▶ Outline

I. Greeting and Prayer (1:1–11)

II. Encouragement about His Imprisonment (1:12–30)

    A. Paul's imprisonment has meant progress for the gospel (1:12–18)

    B. Christ will be magnified in Paul's life or death (1:19–26)

    C. Exhortation to walk worthy of the gospel (1:27–30)

III. Exhortation to Humble Service (2:1–30)

    A. A call to unity, humility, and service to one another (2:1–4)

    B. Christ's example of humble service (2:5–11)

    C. Living as lights in the world (2:12–18)

    D. The Faithful Examples of Timothy and Epaphroditus (2:19–30)

IV. Warning about Distortions of the Gospel (3:1–21)

    A. Contrast between false teachers and the true people of God (3:1–3)

    B. Contrast between self-righteousness and receiving Christ's righteousness (3:4–11)

    C. Paul's progress in the pursuit of Christ (3:12–16)

    D. Contrast between earthly-mindedness and heavenly-mindedness (3:17–21)

V. Concluding Exhortations and Thanksgiving (4:1–23)

    A. A call to unity (4:1–3)

    B. A call to rejoice, trust, pray, and think rightly (4:4–9)

    C. Thanksgiving for the Philippians' gift; Paul's contentment in God (4:10–20)

    D. Greetings and benediction (4:21–23)

As You Get Started . . .

Read the book through in one sitting. Then, more slowly, read the verses that were referenced in the Getting Acquainted section of this lesson.

What do you think is unique about the book of Philippians?

Which themes stood out to you?

Which passages or ideas did you find confusing?

As You Finish This Unit . . .

Take a moment now to ask the Lord to work in your heart and mind through the rest of this study in Philippians.

Definitions

[1] **Messiah** – Transliteration of a Hebrew word meaning "anointed one," the equivalent of the Greek word *Christ*. Originally applied to anyone specially designated for a particular role, such as king or priest. In Jesus' day, the word denoted the liberator-king for whom all the Jews were waiting. Jesus himself affirmed that he was the Messiah sent from God (Matt. 16:16–17).

[2] **Church** – From a Greek word meaning "assembly." The body of believers in Jesus Christ, referring either to all believers everywhere or to a local gathering of believers.

Week 2: Thankfulness and Prayer for the Philippians

Philippians 1:1–11

▲

The Place of the Passage

Paul begins Philippians much as he does his other letters: a quick salutation, an expression of thankfulness, and a prayer. Within these first 11 verses there are hints of what's to come in the rest of the epistle.[1] That was a common structure for letter writing in Paul's time.

The Big Picture

Paul celebrates God's genuine work of grace in the Philippians, warmly thanking them for their partnership in the gospel, and praying for their future growth in the faith.

Reflection and Discussion

Read through the passage for this study, Philippians 1:1–11. Then consider and answer the following questions. (For further background, see the *ESV Study Bible*, pages 2280–2281, or visit esv.org.)

Knowing what you do about the major themes of Philippians (see Week 1), read verses 1–11 with those in mind. Do you see any ways in which these verses foreshadow what's to come in the rest of the letter?

Paul addresses this letter to "all the saints in Christ Jesus . . . with the overseers and deacons" (v. 1). Look at the first couple of verses in other letters that Paul wrote to churches, such as Romans through 2 Thessalonians. What is unique about how he addresses the Philippians? What might be behind this?

Paul's various arrests, imprisonments, and trials stretch through eight chapters in the book of Acts (Acts 21–28). He writes Philippians while imprisoned and with execution looming. Amazingly, his focus is squarely on the Philippians' welfare. Do you see any indication in verses 1–11 as to why and how Paul can focus on thankfulness, joy, and the welfare of others, instead of on his own hard circumstances?

Paul's language is extremely warm and personal in these verses (especially vv. 3–5, 7–8). Why? Was it mere courtesy? Was it based on time spent together? Or was there a still deeper connection? (Hint: notice the connecting language in vv. 5, 7, which introduces his stated reasons—e.g., "because . . . ," "It is right . . . because . . . ," "for . . .")

The Greek word behind "partnership" (v. 5) is sometimes translated "fellowship." Unfortunately, for many Christians today "fellowship" has connotations of merely getting together for food. So "partnership" is a better word, especially here. Remember, the Philippians prayerfully and financially supported Paul's missionary work. They shared the *gospel* and shared in *gospel work* (see 3 John 6–8 for similar language). Remarkably, they even indirectly shared in Paul's "imprisonment and . . . defense and confirmation of the gospel" (v. 7). What are some implications of this for you, your church, your giving, etc.?

In verse 6, Paul assures the Philippians that their spiritual state is proof of God's "good work" in them. He also insists that if God "began a good work" in them, he "will bring it to completion." How might these statements be simultaneously *confidence-building* and *pride-crushing*?

List some of the things that Paul is thankful for in the Philippians, in verses 3–7, and the things that he prays for them, in verses 9–11. Then read Paul's prayers in Ephesians 1:15–23, Colossians 1:9–14, and 2 Thessalonians 1:3–12. What similarities do you see among these prayers?

Having looked at several of Paul's prayers, what things do you see Paul emphasizing in his prayers? What *kinds* of things is he praying for? Why? How might Paul's prayers differ from our prayers?

Read through the following three sections on *Gospel Glimpses, Whole-Bible Connections*, and *Theological Soundings*. Then take time to consider the *Personal Implications* these sections may have for you.

Gospel Glimpses

SALVATION BELONGS TO THE LORD. That is what Jonah concluded after God sent him to the Ninevites to preach repentance and had him swallowed by a fish when he ran away from the task (Jonah 2:9). God's saving plan for them and for us began in eternity past (Eph. 1:4–5). Salvation starts with God, not us. If left to ourselves, we would never seek God (Rom. 3:11). Paul was not in search of Jesus that day on the road to Damascus; Jesus went looking for him (Acts 9:1–6). So too the Philippian Gentiles were not searching for the true God when the gospel was first preached in their city (Acts 16). Lydia, though religious, believed Paul's message only because the Lord "opened her heart" (v. 14). The same is true of you, if you're a Christian: it was God who *began* the work in you, and thus it is he who will surely *complete* it (Phil. 1:6).

SUPERNATURAL CONFIDENCE, JOY, AND LOVE. Especially in light of his many persecutions and present imprisonment, it is astounding how steadily joy-filled, thankful, and selfless Paul is in Philippians. As we shall see throughout Philippians, these were supernatural realities for Paul, attitudes tied to his experience of God's grace and the innumerable benefits that were his in Christ. His confidence and joy were rooted in eternal truths, not mere circumstances. He was unswervingly confident because Christ is unshakably faithful. And Paul was effervescent in his love for other believers because the gospel showed him Christ's love and taught him to love in imitation of it.

▶ Whole-Bible Connections

THE DAY OF JESUS CHRIST. Paul assured the Philippian church that their salvation would be brought to completion "at the day of Jesus Christ" (1:6). He also prayed that the Philippians would be found "pure and blameless" in "the day of Christ" (1:10). For hundreds of years before Jesus' birth, the Old Testament promised the hastening of this day—"the day of the LORD" (Isa. 13:6; Joel 2:1; Amos 5:18). The prophets spoke of this "day" sometimes as a day of *salvation* and sometimes as a day of *judgment*. The New Testament reflects this distinction. In Acts 2:16–21 Peter insists that the "last days," spoken of by Joel, have now come with Jesus and his Spirit. In that sense, the "day of the Lord" has already come. However, the apostles also wrote of this "day" as still a future event (Phil. 1:6; 1 Thess. 5:2; 2 Pet. 3:10). This is the day of Jesus' return, his second coming. Just as the cross was a day of *salvation* and *judgment* (as Jesus paid for mankind's sins by bearing God's wrath), so his second coming will also be a day of final *salvation* for some and final *judgment* for others (2 Thess. 1:7–10).

FOR GOD'S GLORY AND PRAISE. God saves us for his "glory and praise" (Phil. 1:11). Paul uses the words *glory* and *praise* like a repeated chorus in Ephesians. There he writes that our adoption is "to the praise of his glorious grace" (Eph. 1:6) and our inheritence and saving hope are "to the praise of his glory" (vv. 11–12). Of course, this is not unique to Paul or the New Testament. It was clear throughout the Old Testament that *glory* and *praise* are, and always were, integral to God's character, and, hence, integral to his plan. For instance, he said through the prophet Isaiah, "For my name's sake I defer my anger, for the sake of my *praise* I restrain it for you" (Isa. 48:9). This will also be the eternal anthem of heaven: "Let us rejoice and exult and give him the glory" (Rev. 19:7).

Theological Soundings

PRAYER. What is prayer? On one level, prayer is simply talking to God about what is in one's mind at the moment. But on a deeper level, there are many things going on that are very theological because they are essentially responses to God. For starters, prayer is possible only because of the intricate, eternal, historical plan of God to save sinners in and through Jesus. Prayer is speaking to God in praise about who he is—and he is infinitely glorious. Prayer is thanking him for what he has done—and he has done innumerably wonderful things. Prayer is speaking to God about his plan, asking him to do what he promised to do. Paul's prayer in Philippians 1 is a model of a loving, worshipful, thoughtful, God-centered prayer. In many ways, he simply fleshes out what our Lord taught us to pray: that God's name would be hallowed, his kingdom keep coming, his will be done, and we be kept from temptation (Matt. 6:9–13).

PERSERVERANCE OF THE SAINTS.[2] Paul assures the Philippian church that the saving work that God began in them would be brought "to completion at the day of . . . Christ" (Phil. 1:6), and he also *prays* for the same (v. 10). In the following chapter, he speaks of the same concept in a slightly different way: he prays that the Philippians will always be found "holding fast to the word of life, so that in the day of Christ" he would not prove to have "run in vain" (2:16). These verses reflect a tension between God's sovereignty and human responsibility that is felt all through Philippians (see also, e.g., 2:12–13). On the one hand, God will powerfully preserve all true believers to the end. On the other hand, those very same believers have a genuine responsibility to hold fast to the word, to see to it that they not "run in vain." That's why Paul assures the Philippians that their salvation is as good as done yet also prays for that very thing and bids them to stand firm in it (1:27).

Personal Implications

Take time to reflect on the implications of Philippians 1:1–11 for your own life today. Consider what you have learned that might lead you to praise God, repent of sin, and trust in his gracious promises. Make notes below on the personal implications for your walk with the Lord of the (1) *Gospel Glimpses*, (2) *Whole-Bible Connections*, (3) *Theological Soundings*, and (4) this passage as a whole.

1. Gospel Glimpses

2. Whole-Bible Connections

3. Theological Soundings

4. Philippians 1:1–11

As You Finish This Unit . . .

Take a moment now to ask for the Lord's blessing and help as you continue in this study of Philippians. And take a moment also to look back through this unit of study, to reflect on a few key things that the Lord may be teaching you—and perhaps to highlight and underline these things to review again in the future.

Definitions

[1] **Epistle** – Essentially synonymous with "letter." A literary form common in NT times. Epistles typically included: (1) statement of author and recipient; (2) brief greetings and expressions of thanks; (3) the body of the letter; (4) personal greetings and signature; and (5) a closing doxology or blessing. Twenty-one books of the NT are epistles.

[2] **Perseverance of the Saints** – According to this doctrine, God enables all true believers to remain faithful to the end. Those who willfully continue in sin reveal that they were never truly believers. Others may for a time *appear* to abandon their faith though they have not in fact done so. This doctrine does not deny the reality that even true believers still sin, nor does it mean that those who have made a profession of faith are free to live sinful, godless lives.

WEEK 3: PAUL'S IMPRISONMENT IS FOR THE GREATER GOOD

Philippians 1:12–18

▲

▶ The Place of the Passage

After Paul's introductory words of greeting and thankfulness, he turns to one of his main purposes in writing this letter: to update the Philippian church on his welfare—"I want you to know . . . what has happened to me" (Phil. 1:12). They were concerned for Paul in these days of imprisonment. In 1:12–26 Paul seeks to assure them, first with news that the gospel is spreading (1:12–18), then by modeling confidence in God's sovereignty[1] over life and death (1:19–26).

▶ The Big Picture

In Philippians 1:12–18 Paul encourages the church with the news that the gospel is spreading, not despite his imprisonment but *through* it—and this is all that matters.

▶ Reflection and Discussion

Read through the passage for this study, Philippians 1:12–18. Then consider and answer the following questions. (For further background, see the *ESV Study Bible*, page 2281, or visit esv.org.)

Verse 12 begins with the words, "I want you to know . . ." What might this phrase indicate about this section of Philippians? What might it suggest about Paul's purposes in this letter?

If the phrase "I want you to know" (v. 12) begins a new section of Philippians, where does that section end? Or, put another way, which verses in chapter 1 fall under that introductory phrase "I want you to know" (v. 12)? (Hint: it may go beyond the verses for this chapter of the study guide.)

Paul encourages the concerned Philippians by insisting that his imprisonment has actually helped the spread of the gospel, and he gives three examples to prove his point (vv. 12–18). Identify each of the encouraging examples, describing them in your own words. (Hint: one is in vv. 12–13, another in v. 14, and another in vv. 15–18).

Isn't it wonderfully ironic how *opposition to* the gospel could turn into *opportunities for* the gospel? That certainly wasn't coincidence or luck; God was behind it all. As with Joseph's brothers, what Paul's enemies meant for evil, "God meant . . . for good" (Gen. 50:20). Can you think of other stories in Scripture where something was meant for evil but used by God for good? After answering that question, read Acts 2:23 and 4:27 for the ultimate instance of this.

In verses 14–16 Paul mentions several good and right motivations for preaching the gospel. Identify them, noting also the wrong motivations Paul mentions in verses 15–17.

Paul says that his imprisonment for Christ has actually made some believers more "confident" and "much more bold to speak the word without fear" (v. 14). This may seem counterintuitive. Why would persecution of one Christian produce courage in others? What does "love" (v. 16) have to do with gospel-boldness?

In verses 15–17 Paul talks about a strange kind of Christian preacher: they "preach Christ" out of "envy and rivalry . . . out of selfish ambition . . . to afflict"

Paul. It is difficult for us to understand exactly who these people were and how they could oppose Paul *by* preaching Christ, though rivalry among preachers is not unknown. Without perhaps coming to a full understanding of what was going on, write down what can be known about these preachers, their motives, and their message. (See p. 2281 of the *ESV Study Bible* if you need help.)

What do verses 12–18 say about Paul's priorities, aims, concerns, and joys? What is primary in Paul's mind, according to these verses? Which verse makes that explicit?

Paul joyfully celebrates the gospel's advance (v. 12) through Christ being preached (v. 18). Is this just his own personal testimony to the Philippians, or something more? Is he simply informing them, or implying something more for them? What is he *saying without saying it*?

Read through the following three sections on *Gospel Glimpses*, *Whole-Bible Connections*, and *Theological Soundings*. Then take time to consider the *Personal Implications* these sections may have for you.

Gospel Glimpses

A CONVICTING EXAMPLE, A COMFORTING GOSPEL. Paul's singularly focused concern for the cause of Christ and his gospel is in sharp contrast to our puny efforts and quick complaints. Paul's radical example is convicting. That is not an inappropriate response. God is good when his Word exposes our sin and draws us into repentant confession and humility. We should be reproved by Paul's bold example. But we should also be comforted by the very gospel he so radically preached. Jesus died for sins, including the sins of cowardice, selfishness, joylessness, and complaining. This is the gospel that we have heard and believed and received as Christians. Paul provides a lofty, convicting example, but he too is motivated by a gloriously comforting gospel.

THE GOSPEL IS FREEING AND FIXATING. In the midst of imprisonment and opposition, Paul's joy (1:18) is otherworldly. Only the gospel can free us from focusing on our circumstances and then fixate our hearts on Christ and his cause in this world. Paul shows us the power of the gospel to bring supernatural joy because of spiritual realties. As he wrote to the Corinthians, "we look not to the things that are seen but to the things that are unseen. For the things that are seen are transient, but the things that are unseen are eternal" (2 Cor. 4:18).

Whole-Bible Connections

THE ADVANCE OF THE GOSPEL. The gospel is supposed to spread. It is good news to be proclaimed freely, widely, and boldly. Jesus issued this call to his followers multiple times (Matt. 28:18–20; Luke 24:47–48; Acts 1:8). But the idea of salvation spreading in the world was promised and foreshadowed all through the Old Testament, beginning with God's promises to Abraham (see Gen. 12:3). Throughout the Old Testament God had a unique covenantal relationship with the nation of Israel, but all along there was a growing anticipation that God's saving program would eventually reach the Gentile nations; one day "the earth will be filled with the knowledge of the glory of the LORD" (Hab. 2:14). Very early in Jesus' earthly ministry he made it clear that this time of globally spreading glory had begun. He came not for the "righteous," but for "sinners" (Luke 5:32)—regardless of their ethnicity. This Old Testament background combined with Jesus' model and teaching formed Paul's aim to "preach the gospel, not where Christ has already been named" (Rom. 15:20). That is why he preached the gospel in Philippi (Acts 16:11–34), and why he eventually left Philippi for the next city. That is why he rejoiced in his Roman imprisonment and the spread of the gospel among Roman guards (Phil. 1:12–13).

OPPOSITION TO THE GOSPEL. God's redemptive plan for the nations is not always met with belief and joy. Paul wrote Philippians while imprisoned for Christ. The frequency and severity of the persecution he had previously faced was simply remarkable (read 2 Cor. 11:23–27). But it was not surprising in light of Jesus' opposition and cruel death (John 15:20). Like the *advance* of the gospel, *opposition* to it has a long history in the Bible. That's why the early church, when persecuted and threatened, looked back to Psalm 2 to remember the promise of human opposition to God's ways and to encourage themselves by dwelling on the futility of that opposition (Acts 4:25–28). The coming of the true, anointed King inevitably results in both salvation and opposition.

Theological Soundings

THE GOSPEL.[2] The word "gospel," the basic label for Paul's message, is used throughout Philippians. More often, though, the concept of the gospel is put in slightly different terms. For instance, it is "the word" in 1:14 and simply "Christ" in 1:15, 17, and 18. These different words shed light on what the gospel is. It is "good news," a "word" to "speak" (v. 14), to "preach" (v. 15), to be "proclaimed" (vv. 17–18). More specifically, it is an announcement of a person—Christ, the Messiah. More specifically still, it regards his *person* and *work*: that he lived righteously, died horribly, and rose victoriously for the salvation of his people. Our hope is completely and solely in him. This is good news to be heard, embraced, celebrated, and retold.

SOVEREIGNTY AND PROVIDENCE.[3] Not once in this passage does Paul say explicitly that God has sovereignly placed him in prison for his good and for the gospel's spread. There's no need to say this; it is obvious. God sovereignly orchestrated the evil of men and the gospel-passion of Christians for a gospel-spreading good that no one could plan or stumble into. The doctrine of God's sovereignty insists that God is in complete control of everything. The overlapping doctrine of God's providence teaches that God is good, wise, and purposeful in his sovereignty; his plan is for our good and his glory. Paul's imprisonment is an example of these things, but Jesus' death is the ultimate instance. Though "killed by the hands of lawless men," he was "delivered up according to the definite plan and foreknowledge of God" (Acts 2:23). His crucifiers plotted in vain, for they did only what God himself "had predestined to take place" (Acts 4:25–28).

Personal Implications

Take time to reflect on the implications of Philippians 1:12–18 for your own life today. Consider what you have learned that might lead you to praise God, repent of sin, and trust in his gracious promises. Make notes below on the personal implicacations for your walk with the Lord of the (1) *Gospel Glimpses*, (2) *Whole-Bible Connections*, (3) *Theological Soundings*, and (4) this passage as a whole.

1. Gospel Glimpses

2. Whole-Bible Connections

3. Theological Soundings

4. Philippians 1:12–18

> ## As You Finish This Unit . . .

Take a moment now to ask for the Lord's blessing and help as you continue in this study of Philippians. And take a moment also to look back through this unit of study, to reflect on a few key things that the Lord may be teaching you—and perhaps to highlight and underline these things to review again in the future.

Definitions

[1] **Sovereignty** – Supreme and independent power and authority. Sovereignty over all things is a distinctive attribute of God (1 Tim. 6:15–16). He directs all things to carry out his purposes (Rom. 8:28–29).

[2] **Gospel** – A common translation for a Greek word meaning "good news," that is, the good news of Jesus Christ and the salvation he made possible by his crucifixion, burial, and resurrection. *Gospel* with an initial capital letter refers to each of the biblical accounts of Jesus' life on earth (Matthew, Mark, Luke, and John).

[3] **Providence** – God's good, wise, and sovereign guidance and control of all things, by which he supplies all our needs and accomplishes his holy will.

WEEK 4: WHETHER IN LIFE OR DEATH, CHRIST WILL BE MAGNIFIED

Philippians 1:19–30

The Place of the Passage

Having assured the concerned Philippians that his imprisonment has turned out for the good of the gospel (1:12–18), Paul continues with still another section under the heading "I want you to know . . ." (v. 12). He was likely aware of questions the Philippians had been entertaining and praying about (v. 19): e.g., Will Paul's imprisonment end in freedom or in execution? Will they see him again? How should they pray for him? Paul's response (vv. 19–26) to those kinds of questions has been variously understood, but it is clear that he meant to give comfort, encouragement, and also subtle correction. The chapter closes by exhorting the Philippians to stand firm and united (vv. 27–30), themes which he expounds in chapter 2.

The Big Picture

Paul seeks to assuage the Philippians' concerns for his well-being, not with a simple assurance that his circumstances will turn out fine, but by demonstrating his own trust in God and by calling them to the same level of trust.

Reflection and Discussion

Read through the full passage for this study, Philippians 1:19–30. Then prayerfully consider and answer the following questions. (For further background, see the *ESV Study Bible*, pages 2281–2282, or visit esv.org.)

As noted above, verses 19–26 have been variously interpreted and are difficult to understand. At times Paul seems to say that he knows that his imprisonment will not end in death but in freedom, and that he will return to Philippi. Other times he seems quite unsure about his fate. Identify the verses and language in each of those two categories.

An important clue in understanding these difficult verses is to know that in verse 19 Paul alludes to Job 13:13–18 (especially v. 16). Read Job 13:13–18 and note any parallels you see with Philippians 1:19–26.

Paul's confidence for "deliverance" (v. 19) mirrors Job's confidence in "salvation" (Job 13:16). Should we assume that Paul and Job are thinking of the same kind of deliverance/salvation? If so, what kind of deliverance/salvation do they have in mind? Temporary or eternal? (Hint: note the similar language in Paul's final letter recorded in Scripture; 2 Tim. 4:18.)

What, precisely, does Paul say is his "eager expectation and hope" (v. 20)?

Notice that the final words of verse 20 become the major themes of verses 21–24. What is the relationship between verse 20 and the few verses that follow? Put another way, what is Paul doing in verses 21–24 that he hasn't done in verse 20? (See p. 2281 of the ESV Study Bible for help.)

If verses 19–20 express Paul's confidence in his eternal salvation, and if verses 21–23 clarify that death is no threat to that saving hope, how should we understand Paul's confidence that he will "remain and continue" in verses 24–26? What might he be reassuring them of or clarifying for them in verses 24–26?

In verses 25–26, Paul sounds quite certain of his release from prison and his return to Philippi. But read on in chapter 1. Is the apparent certainty of verses 25–26 confirmed or qualified? Which verse tells us this?

Paul clearly feels torn between living and dying, between the ongoing needs of the church and the glory of Christ in heaven (vv. 22–24). But which of the two possibilities would he prefer, all things considered? What language does Paul use about his preferred outcome?

Paul speaks of death in optimistic terms (vv. 21–23). That path is "gain" and "far better." Paul doesn't explicitly tell us why in this passage; he merely assumes the reasons. From what you know of the Bible, what are some ways in which dying is "gain" for the believer?

Likewise, in what ways is dying *far* from "gain" for those outside of Christ?

The alternative to death—to "remain in the flesh" (v. 24)—certainly has its own benefits and purposes. How does Paul describe that outcome in verses 20–26? Or, how does he view his life? How might Paul's aims relate to the two great commands in Matthew 22:36–40?

In a footnote, the ESV notes that the phrase "let your manner of life be worthy" (v. 27) can be more literally translated "behave as citizens worthy." Notice that in 3:20 Paul similarly says "our citizenship is in heaven." That word "citizen" is rich with significance. Why? List some dynamics of citizenship that Paul intends for his readers to apply to their Christian lives.

Within his commands, Paul gives encouragements or reasons to more fully embrace that path (see vv. 28b–30). What are they?

Read through the following three sections on *Gospel Glimpses*, *Whole-Bible Connections*, and *Theological Soundings*. Then take time to consider the *Personal Implications* these sections may have for you.

Gospel Glimpses

TO DIE IS TO GAIN. Death can only be gain if what is on the other side is of greater value than anything on this side. In his death and victorious resurrection, Jesus "abolished death and brought life and immortality to light through the gospel" (2 Tim. 1:10). He died so that "through death he might destroy the one who has the power of death, that is, the devil, and deliver all those who through fear of death were subject to lifelong slavery" (Heb. 2:14–15). Death is as good as dead. It is not fully dead yet—obvious enough since we still die (see 1 Cor. 15:25–26). But for the Christian, death is nothing more than a passageway to another stage of redemption, to more of Christ's presence, to the absence of sin and sickness and pain. So even now we can say with Paul, "Death is swallowed up in victory. O death, where is your victory? O death, where is your sting?" (1 Cor. 15:54–55). Jesus defeated death. Now, death is gain.

PROGRESS AND JOY IN THE FAITH. If Paul is given life beyond his imprisonment, and is able to return to Philippi, he envisions that his ministry among the Philippians will be for their "progress and joy in the faith" (v. 25). That phrase, in many ways, captures the essence of the Christian life. It is one of progress, of growing. As Paul will later say, we are to "work out . . . salvation" (2:12) and "press on toward the goal . . . of the upward call" (3:14). But this "progress" is not merely an improved performance or deeper knowledge. Conduct and knowledge are certainly involved, but at the root, Paul insists that we are to progress "in the *faith*"—in the gospel. It is not something we move beyond after we've received it; we live, and relate to God, the Father, the Son, and the Spirit, first to last, in light of the gospel.

Whole-Bible Connections

TO BE WITH CHRIST. God's plan can be charted through a lens of his presence among his people. The garden of Eden was a place of his presence, the first couple in perfect communion with him. But after their sin, Adam and Eve hid from God. God came calling for them, but that conversation ended with them being cast out of the garden. In time, God spoke to Noah, then to Abraham and his offspring, but these were not frequent or constant experiences. God spoke more frequently to Moses, but it wasn't until after the exodus that God began to be "in the midst" of the people (see Ex. 25:8). The tabernacle was a place for his dwelling; the temple would be his more permanent house in the Promised Land. God's people have always fearfully but joyfully longed for his presence (Ps. 16:11)—and indeed granting this has been God's plan. That's why Jesus "tabernacled" among us (John 1:14); why he later gave us his Spirit to dwell in our hearts; and why Jesus will come again—that we might be fully with him and see his glory (John 17:24). And *that* is why Paul could say, to "be with Christ" would be "far better" (Phil. 1:23).

BETWEEN TWO WORLDS. Paul was a man with one foot planted on earth and another planted in heaven.[1] He lived at the same time in this world and in the world to come. This is apparent as he wrestles with conflicting desires— wanting to depart from this world to be with Jesus, and yet feeling the need to remain in this world for the sake of the church. We too should see that needs are many and there is much work to be done for Jesus and his church. But, like Paul, we too should have a constant eye on, even a sincere longing for, what's to come, whether at the time of our death or at Jesus' return.

Theological Soundings

SUFFERING *FOR* CHRIST VERSUS SUFFERING *WITH* CHRIST. Paul was clear that only Christ's suffering secures our salvation. In fact, he had strong words for false teachers who insisted on self-induced suffering as a form of religion (see Col. 2:18–23). That said, in Philippians 1, he insists that those who savingly know Christ's suffering *for them*, will also willingly embrace suffering *for him*. It "is a clear sign . . . of your salvation," and it is "from God" (Phil. 1:28). We've been "granted . . . not only [to] believe in him, but also [to] suffer for his sake" (v. 29). This kind of suffering for Christ is not a saving suffering; it is not penance or paying off guilt. But it does have great value. It gives assurance to us and confirmation to the world that we belong to and follow Christ. Further, as Paul insists later in Philippians and elsewhere, suffering for Christ is a special kind of identification with him; in that sense, we "share in his sufferings" (Phil. 3:10; Rom. 8:17; 2 Cor. 1:5).

WORTHY OF THE GOSPEL. Paul exhorts[2] the Philippians, "let your manner of life be worthy of the gospel" (v. 27). Paul is not suggesting that the gospel can be earned with a worthy life. No one, in this life or the next, will be "worthy of the gospel" in that sense. The gospel is good news about Someone else's worth and work. What then does Paul mean by his call to a "manner of life" that is "worthy of the gospel"? As noted above, this phrase "manner of life" can be translated "life as *citizens*." It is a word picture that is grasped in any culture that has citizenship, but it would have been especially forceful to people in a city such as Philippi, most of whom were Roman citizens. To be a Roman citizen didn't just mean that you were born in a Roman province. It was to be *Roman*—with Roman thinking, Roman ways, Roman culture, and Roman allegiances (especially to Caesar). Paul is shaking all that up by directing their focus to a higher citizenship, higher identity, higher standard of conduct, and higher allegiance. They are now to live in a way that befits—that is "worthy of"—the gospel and this heavenly citizenship.

▶ Personal Implications

Take time to reflect on the implications of Philippians 1:19–30 for your own life today. Consider what you have learned that might lead you to praise God, repent of sin, and trust in his gracious promises. Make notes below on the personal implications for your walk with the Lord of the (1) *Gospel Glimpses*, (2) *Whole-Bible Connections*, (3) *Theological Soundings*, and (4) this passage as a whole.

1. Gospel Glimpses

2. Whole-Bible Connections

3. Theological Soundings

4. Philippians 1:19–30

> ### As You Finish This Unit . . .

Take a moment now to ask for the Lord's blessing and help as you continue in this study of Philippians. And take a moment also to look back through this unit of study, to reflect on a few key things that the Lord may be teaching you—and perhaps to highlight and underline these things to review again in the future.

Definitions

[1] **Heaven** – The sky, or the abode of God (Matt. 6:9), which is commonly regarded as being above the earth and sky. As the abode of God, heaven is also the place where believers live in God's presence after death (1 Thess. 4:16–17).

[2] **Exhortation** – A message encouraging someone to follow a particular course of action or to submit to a different way of thinking.

Week 5: A Call to Humble Sacrifice; Jesus' Supreme Example

Philippians 2:1–11

The Place of the Passage

After almost a full chapter of thanking and comforting the Philippian church, Paul turned in Philippians 1:27 to some direct exhortations or commands. As we noted in the last section, unity is central to the exhortations ending chapter 1. In chapter 2, Paul's exhortations continue, as does the major theme of unity in the church—now with a heightened appeal, with more specificity, and with motivation added to the general commands of 1:27. Paul will return to the theme of unity again in chapter 4. Unity is clearly a major theme of this letter, but 2:1–11 is the linchpin holding it all together.

The Big Picture

On the basis of the rich realities of the gospel, Paul commands the church to be unified by being humble and caring, looking to Christ as the perfect example of humble servanthood in his incarnation, crucifixion, and exaltation.

Reflection and Discussion

Read through the complete passage for this study, Philippians 2:1–11. Then review the questions below concerning this section of Paul's letter and write your notes on them. (For further background, see the *ESV Study Bible*, pages 2282–2283, or visit esv.org.)

Paul will go on in verses 2 and following to call the Philippians to specific ways to strive for unity and peace. But first, in verse 1, he begins by establishing four fundamental realities of being in Christ. Why do you think Paul did this before telling them what to do in verses 2ff.?

How do the four conditions of verse 1 relate to what follows in verses 2–8? Notice that Paul is speaking in personal, experiential, "vertical" ways (one's relationship to the gospel and God) in verse 1, but does that very language also hint at "horizontal" implications? How?

Notice that little word "if" at the beginning of verse 1. What is the significance of the word in this context? How might it relate to assurance of salvation? Does it signify that Paul is skeptical about the genuineness of the Philippians' faith? Is there anything in chapter 1 that helps us answer this question?

Paul has already expressed his general desire for the church to "progress" in their joy and faith (1:25). In chapter 2 he calls them to progress in specific ways: "being of the same mind, having the same love," etc. (v. 2). But, technically, these aren't the *commands* of verse 2. His command is that they would "complete my joy." What does it say about Paul's heart, leadership, and personal connection to the Philippians that he couches his call to unity in a call to "complete [his] joy"?

Verse 2 contains four different phrases describing unity. There is distinctiveness and overlap in each phrase. Notice that Paul seems to stress the unity of *mind* and *truth* in each. What does Paul have in mind with this emphasis? (As you answer, consider Eph. 4:1–6.)

As he moves from verse 2 to verses 3–4, Paul clearly sees personal humility as a necessary ingredient in the church's unity. Such humility is exemplified in a number of different ways. What are they and why are they integral to unity?

What is the relationship between verses 1–5 and verses 6–8? Why does Paul include this thorough description of Jesus' incarnation in verses 6–8 after his call to unity and humility?

With all of the rich theological language of verses 6–8, Paul's primary point may be slightly overlooked. It is a point about servanthood and service. The word "servant" (v. 7) is a good summary of these verses, tethering the rich theological language to Paul's main point in verses 1–8. In what ways was Jesus a "servant"?

After unpacking Christ's humility in the servanthood of the incarnation and the cross, Paul turns in verses 9–11 to Jesus' subsequent exaltation. Why do you think he added that? Is Christ's exaltation also in some way exemplary for the Philippians, or is it just a necessary completion of Christ's personal story?

Read through the following three sections on *Gospel Glimpses, Whole-Bible Connections*, and *Theological Soundings*. Then take time to consider the *Personal Implications* these sections may have for you.

AN EXAMPLE, BUT MORE THAN AN EXAMPLE. Those familiar with Philippians 2 may think of the rich Christology of verses 6–11 apart from the context and Paul's aims in the passage. Though these verses are important for our understanding of Christ's deity, humanity, incarnation,[1] etc., Paul's primary goal here is to show Jesus as the ultimate example of humility, servanthood, and sacrifice. It is "this mind" that we should have among ourselves (v. 5). So too, elsewhere in Scripture, Jesus' life and death are an "example" to his followers (John 13:15; 1 Pet. 2:21). And yet it is crucial that Christians never begin to think of Jesus' cross as *merely* an example. For those who have received his free and deep grace, gratitude and awe are never far from their minds. They cannot read words like those in Philippians 2:6–11 without remembering the servanthood and sacrifice of the cross that was on *their behalf* and in *their place.*

THE GOSPEL'S HORIZONTAL EFFECTS. The four conditions of verse 1 are simply the fundamental realities of the gospel; they are inevitable results of being "in Christ."[2] But Paul sees these as bases for his call to peace and oneness with others (v. 2). This suggests that the gospel doesn't merely forgive, or even merely restore us to fellowship with God. It also changes us from the inside out and unites us to others in Christ's body. Because we have Christ's *encouragement, comfort,* and *love*; because we share the *Spirit*; because we each have God's *affection* and *sympathy*, we are "one" in Christ. To be sure, our sinful, selfish selves often get in the way of living that out fully. That's why Paul wrote these words to the Philippians, and why we still need them today. But the basis and power for pursuing further unity with others is in the gospel, with its manifold benefits.

JESUS, THE SUFFERING SERVANT. Paul's teaching on Christ's humble, servant-like sacrifice has its roots in the Old Testament theme of "the servant of the Lord" (Isaiah 42; 49; 53). While not quoting directly from key passages like Isaiah 53, Paul clearly alludes to Isaiah's "suffering servant." Though he was eternally and fully God—with all divine rights, privileges, and attributes—the second person of the Trinity took on flesh and was born (Phil. 2:6). In doing so, he "emptied himself" and took on the "form of a servant" (v. 7). The extent of his servanthood was complete—unto death. Further, Paul specifies that his death was "on a cross" (v. 8)—a form of death that uniquely fits the graphically violent language of Isaiah 53. Paul, then, isn't just reminding the Philippians what happened or what Jesus did but is reminding them also *who he is*: the Promised One, the Messiah, the fulfillment.

JESUS, THE EXALTED LORD. Philippians 2:9–11 explains one major outcome of Christ's righteous suffering and death: the Father exalted Jesus. In the resurrection, and later in the ascension, Christ's deity, obedience, and sacrificial death were vindicated by God. The themes of vindication and exaltation are likewise part of those servant passages in Isaiah. God will "prolong his days; the will of the LORD shall prosper in his hand. Out of the anguish of his soul, he shall see and be satisfied" (Isa. 53:10–11). God's servant "shall be high and lifted up, and shall be exalted" (52:13). Paul also insists that this exaltation resulted in Christ bearing "the name that is above every name" (Phil. 2:9). He is "LORD"—a term that reflects not only authority but also God's personal name, *Yahweh* (Isa. 42:8). Before this name, "every knee should bow ... and every tongue confess" (Phil. 2:10–11). Paul takes these phrases from Isaiah 45:23, thereby equating the servant Christ with Yahweh himself.

▶ Theological Soundings

JESUS' ETERNALITY AND DEITY.[3] As discussed in the previous paragraph, Christ's deity is unmistakable in the exaltation language of Philippians 2:9–11. However, Paul's earlier words about Christ's preincarnate state also stress his deity. He was "in the form of God" (v. 6)—not that he had some Godlike qualities or appearance, but that he was of the same nature or essence. He "did not count equality with God a thing to be grasped" (v. 6)—a thing to attain or reach—since equality with God was already his. Paul mentions no starting point for this divine status; it is eternally so, just as Jesus himself taught (John 8:58) and Paul elsewhere states (Col. 1:16).

ONE PERSON, TWO NATURES. When Paul writes that Christ "emptied himself" (v. 7), he doesn't mean that Christ emptied himself of divinity, or even of some divine attributes. He is stressing that all divine *privileges*, though rightfully his, were humbly set aside in becoming a man and suffering in our place. Likewise, the language of "taking the *form* of a servant ... being born in the *likeness* of men ... in human *form*" (vv. 7–8) doesn't suggest that Christ was only human-*like* or only *appeared* human. The incarnate Christ was one divine-human person with two natures. The early church rightly discerned[4] that these two natures are united without mixture, confusion, separation, or division. As one person, Jesus did not alternate between his human and divine natures. Instead he operated out of the totality of his divine-human person. While these are profound theological matters, in principle they are simply drawn from and necessitated by the divine-human language of Philippians 2:6–8. (For more on these matters, see the article "The Person of Christ," pp. 2515–2519 in the *ESV Study Bible*.)

▶ **Personal Implications**

Take time to reflect on the implications of Philippians 2:1–11 for your own life today. Consider what you have learned that might lead you to praise God, repent of sin, and trust in his gracious promises. Make notes below on the personal implications for your walk with the Lord of the (1) *Gospel Glimpses*, (2) *Whole-Bible Connections*, (3) *Theological Soundings*, and (4) this passage as a whole.

1. Gospel Glimpses

2. Whole-Bible Connections

3. Theological Soundings

4. Philippians 2:1–11

> **As You Finish This Unit . . .**

Take a moment now to ask for the Lord's blessing and help as you continue in this study of Philippians. And take a moment also to look back through this unit of study, to reflect on a few key things that the Lord may be teaching you—and perhaps to highlight and underline these things to review again in the future.

Definitions

[1] **Incarnation** – Literally "(becoming) in flesh," it refers to God becoming a human being in the person of Jesus of Nazareth.

[2] **Christ** – Transliteration of the Greek for "anointed one" (equivalent to Hebrew Messiah). The term is used throughout the NT as a title for Jesus, indicating his role as Messiah and Savior.

[3] **Deity** – God's unique, essential nature as supreme and eternal. Jesus, the Son of God, possesses deity. He is fully God, as is the Holy Spirit.

[4] **Discernment** – Wisdom in perception and judgment. Spiritual discernment is a Spirit-enabled capacity in believers to understand God's truths (1 Cor. 2:9–16) as well as to identify spiritual error (1 John 4:1–6).

WEEK 6: WORKING *OUT* WHAT GOD HAS WORKED *IN*

Philippians 2:12–18

▲

The Place of the Passage

Having exhorted the Philippians to pursue further unity (1:27–2:4) by looking to Christ as the supreme model of selfless humility (2:5–11), Paul now provides a series of exhortations related to perseverance, especially in light of the watching world (vv. 12–18).

The Big Picture

Paul encourages the Philippians to *work out* the salvation that God is *working in* them, demonstrating the genuineness of their faith to both Paul and the world.

> ### Reflection and Discussion

Read through Philippians 2:12–18, which will be the focus of this week's study. Following this, review the questions below concerning this section of the book of Philippians and write your responses. (For further background, see the *ESV Study Bible*, page 2284, or visit esv.org.)

Paul begins verse 12 with "Therefore…" What follows, then, is the logical outworking of what he said in verses 5–11. But how so? What is the relationship between verses 5–11 and verses 12–18?

The Philippians are called to "work out your own salvation with fear and trembling" (v. 12). This might at first sound like a salvation *by works* instead of *by grace*. But key words in verses 12–13 make it clear that it is not salvation by works. What are those key words, and what do they tell us about what Paul means here?

Verses 12b and 13 are clearly complementary. The first half speaks to human responsibility; the second speaks to God's sovereignty. There is a small connecting word that Paul uses in the middle. What is it and how does it function?

What does "fear and trembling" have to do with *working out your salvation* and *God working in you to will and do*? Describe this "fear and trembling" in your own words, and explain why Paul exhorts Christians in this way.

In verse 14, Paul calls the Philippians to "do all things without grumbling or disputing." Based on what you know of this epistle thus far, in what ways might the Philippians be tempted to grumble or complain? In what ways might they be tempted to dispute or argue?

Recall that Paul began his exhortations in 1:27. He continues this through 2:12–18. Do you see any repeated themes in this broader section? Write down the verses and language that apply. (Hint: start with "disputing" in 2:14 and look for related themes from the earlier verses.)

Of course, "grumbling" and "disputing" (v. 14) are wrong, and that's reason enough for Paul to command the Philippians to forsake such actions and attitudes. But what specific reasons does Paul give in verse 15? How would the sins of "grumbling" and "disputing" stand in the way of Paul's aims for the Philippians, according to these verses?

....

....

....

....

....

....

....

Paul borrows language from Deuteronomy 32:5 when he calls the Philippians to be "children of God without blemish in the midst of a crooked and twisted generation" (v. 15). What themes or words in Philippians 2:12–18 relate to the generation in the wilderness spoken of in Deuteronomy 32:5?

....

....

....

....

....

....

....

Uncertain of his future, Paul again entertains the possibility of martyrdom when he writes of being "poured out as a drink offering" (v. 17). In 1:12–23 Paul gave multiple reasons why he could rejoice in his imprisonment and impending execution. Now in 2:17–18 he gives different reasons for rejoicing. What are they and what do they mean?

....

....

....

....

....

....

....

Read through the following three sections on *Gospel Glimpses, Whole-Bible Connections*, and *Theological Soundings*. Then take time to consider the *Personal Implications* these sections may have for you.

▶ Gospel Glimpses

SALVATION, A FULL PACKAGE. The letter to the Philippians is replete with assurance that when God begins his saving work, he will bring it to completion (1:6). There is a genuine, personal responsibility to *work out* his salvation (i.e., work out the implications more deeply and more broadly in all of life). But even this call is grounded in the reality that God continues to work "in you" (2:12–13). Even more encouraging is the fact that he does this "for [or according to] his good pleasure" (v. 13)—not according to our work or good intentions. He is not limited by us; rather, he enables and empowers us. Paul is explicit: God works in our *wills* and in our *works* (v. 13) And, again, why? Because he wants to! It's his plan and pleasure to do this!

WORKING BECAUSE OF GOD'S WORK. The sovereignty of God's sanctifying work in the Christian is far from a disincentive to our own personal work. God's work is the very basis and primary motivation for ours. It is certainly a mystery precisely how the human responsibility of verse 12 and the divine sovereignty of verse 13 work together, but both are indeed true; both truths are clearly stated. But the word connecting them, "for" (v. 13), is telling, since it speaks to the motivation of our work, or the implication of God's work. God's ongoing, gracious work must not lead to laziness, indifference, or passivity, but to an awe-filled longing and striving to see salvation worked out more broadly and deeply.

▶ Whole-Bible Connections

THE SIN OF GRUMBLING. Paul calls on the church to resist "grumbling" and "disputing" (v. 14). This is one way in which salvation is worked out into the corners of everyday life. But this seemingly simple command also has a missional aim: "that you may be ... without blemish in the midst of a crooked and twisted generation among whom you shine as lights in the world" (v. 15). The absence of complaining and arguing is a testifying mark of those who have put their full trust in the Lord and his plans. Therefore, God takes the sin of grumbling quite seriously. This was a major theme in Israel's years in the wilderness. Not coincidentally, Paul quotes from one of those stories of Israel's grumbling when he exhorts the Philippians to be "without blemish in the midst of a crooked and twisted generation" (see Deut. 32:5). But Paul borrows this language with a twist. Deuteronomy 32:5 spoke of the grumbling *Israelites* as "no longer his children" but rather "blemished" and part of a "crooked and twisted generation." But Paul now calls on the Philippians, as *true* "children of God" (v. 15), to do what Israel did not do: to trust God and not complain or argue. They must be different from Israel of old and the world around them now.

LIGHTS IN THE WORLD. When Paul writes that the Philippians "shine as lights in the world" (Phil. 2:15), he is tapping into rich biblical language. God promised in Isaiah 42:6–7 that he would one day "give a light for the nations, to open the eyes that are blind." The New Testament writers clearly saw this promise fulfilled in the coming of Jesus (Matt. 4:16; Luke 2:32). In fact, Jesus himself insisted that he is "the light of the world" (John 8:12); he came into the world "as light, so that whoever believes" in him will "not remain in darkness" (John 12:46). But Jesus also told his disciples that, by extension, they are "the light of the world." He said, "let your light shine before others, so that they may see your good works and give glory to your Father who is in heaven" (Matt. 5:14–16). Elsewhere in Isaiah, God said he will raise up a people who will be "a light for the nations, that my salvation may reach to the end of the earth" (Isa. 49:6). Paul and Barnabas quote these very words as the basis for their mission to the Gentiles (Acts 13:47). So too the Philippians are to "shine as lights in the world." In short, the Philippians are part of this same great thematic development in God's global saving purposes.

SACRIFICIAL OFFERING. Paul sees his possible martyrdom as a "drink offering" (Phil. 2:17). This is language from the Old Testament Levitical system in which wine was poured onto the ground or an altar as a sacrifice[1] and as a symbol of a life poured out for God. Paul sees his death as worship, as sacrifice, and as a sign of a life fully consecrated to the Lord (see 1:20). Further, he sees the sacrifice of his life as a drink offering which is "*upon* the sacrificial offering of [the Philippians'] faith" (2:17). Their faith and ministry is its own sacrificial offering. Paul's "offering" in death, should *he* soon be martyred, would be a kind of completion of *their* sacrifice (again, see 3 John 6–8).

Theological Soundings

SANCTIFICATION.[2] The Westminster Shorter Catechism from the 1640s explains sanctification as "the work of God's free grace whereby we are renewed in the whole man after the image of God, and are enabled more and more to die unto sin, and live unto righteousness." That's what Paul writes about in Philippians 2:12ff., beginning with a general appeal (vv. 12–13) and moving to specifics like not grumbling (v. 14) but instead rejoicing (v. 18). This is a life-long process, not something immediate or fully achieved in the short term. Sanctification is comprehensive in that it involves the will, actions, and affections. It is not merely moral improvement, not merely "biting the tongue" to hold back grumbling. It is spiritual, even personal. We resist grumbling as "children of God" (v. 15). Sanctification is also gospel-rooted, and yet being *worked out* (v. 12). Thus, there is no real spiritual fight against grumbling or arguing without continually "holding fast to the word of life" (v. 16). It is only this kind of true spiritual transformation that can bring "joy" even in the prospect of a dear friend's impending death (vv. 17–18).

Personal Implications

Take time to reflect on the implications of Philippians 2:12–18 for your own life today. Consider what you have learned that might lead you to praise God, repent of sin, and trust in his gracious promises. Make notes below on the personal implications for your walk with the Lord of the (1) *Gospel Glimpses*, (2) *Whole-Bible Connections*, (3) *Theological Soundings*, and (4) this passage as a whole.

1. Gospel Glimpses

2. Whole-Bible Connections

3. Theological Soundings

4. Philippians 2:12–18

> ## As You Finish This Unit . . .

Take a moment now to ask for the Lord's blessing and help as you continue in this study of Philippians. And take a moment also to look back through this unit of study, to reflect on a few key things that the Lord may be teaching you—and perhaps to highlight and underline these things to review again in the future.

Definitions

[1] **Sacrifice** – An offering to God, often to seek forgiveness of sin. The law of Moses gave detailed instructions regarding various kinds of sacrifices. By his death on the cross, Jesus gave himself as a sacrifice to atone for the sins of believers (Eph. 5:2; Heb. 10:12). Believers are to offer their bodies as living sacrifices to God (Rom. 12:1).

[2] **Sanctification** – The process of being conformed to the image of Jesus Christ through the work of the Holy Spirit. This process begins immediately after regeneration and continues throughout a Christian's life.

WEEK 7: UPDATES, TRAVEL PLANS, AND MODELS TO FOLLOW

Philippians 2:19–30

Personal updates and practical matters are no small part of Paul's letter to the Philippians. In many ways, the letter begins (1:12–18) and ends (4:1–19) on these notes. His update on Timothy and Epaphroditus in the middle (2:19–30) is the longest of these sections. Having called the Philippian church to unity with Christlike selflessness, servanthood, and sacrifice (1:27–2:11), and having commanded them to work out their salvation (2:12–18), Paul now gives necessary updates on two model servants who exemplify the very ideals he has encouraged in 1:27–2:18.

The Big Picture

Knowing their concern for the welfare of their own Epaphroditus, Paul notifies the Philippians of his plans to send back this now-healthy fellow minister and the equally caring Timothy as soon as possible.

Reflection and Discussion

Read through Philippians 2:19–30, which will be the focus of this week's study. Following this, review the questions below concerning this section of the book of Philippians and write your responses. (For further background, see the *ESV Study Bible*, page 2284 or visit esv.org.)

In this passage Paul gives practical updates on the health and the comings and goings of messengers. Such "travelogues" occur in other letters by Paul. Most often they occur at the end of a letter, such as in 2 Timothy 4:9–21. In Philippians, however, this travelogue is in the middle of the body of the letter. Why might this be? What might it signify about 2:19–30?

Read Philippians 4:1–18 with 2:19–30 in mind. Using these passages, and what you know of Paul's situation from earlier in our study, piece together the narrative that is in the background of this letter. In other words, certain events have happened or will happen; what are they? (You should be able to list a half dozen or so.)

Why might Paul have felt the need to keep Timothy with him for the time being (vv. 19–23)? Why might Paul have felt the need to explain to the Philippian church his plans for Timothy?

The apostle Paul had many mission partners and emissaries. In one sense, Timothy was just one of many. But, in another sense, passages like 1 Corinthians 4:16–17 suggest that Timothy was unique. Looking at 1 Corinthians 4:16–17 and Philippians 2:19–26, what words does Paul use to commend Timothy? What words highlight the uniqueness of his relationship to Paul?

Timothy was "genuinely concerned for" the Philippians' "welfare" (v. 20), not like others, who "seek their own interests, not those of Jesus Christ" (v. 21). These are parallel but contrasting statements. What is the connection between the Philippians' "welfare" and the "interests . . . of Jesus Christ"? (Hint: the same parallel is found in Matt. 25:31–46.)

Note the language that Paul uses to describe Timothy and Epaphroditus in 2:19–30. Then reread 2:1–18. What themes and words are in both sections? Is Paul merely acknowledging and commending Timothy and Epaphroditus in verses 19–30, or is he also implying something more?

In verse 25 Paul describes Epaphroditus in five different ways. List them, and then spell each out in your own words.

Epaphroditus's work and worth are spoken of in lofty terms (vv. 25, 29–30). But what was the "work" and "service" that Paul was referring to in verse 30? Are you surprised that such work garners Paul's lofty praise? Why or why not?

Read through the following three sections on *Gospel Glimpses*, *Whole-Bible Connections*, and *Theological Soundings*. Then take time to consider the *Personal Implications* these sections may have for you.

Gospel Glimpses

SEEING CHRIST IN OTHERS. While this section of the letter has its own purposes of updating the Philippians on practical matters, Timothy and Epaphroditus also serve as real-life examples of the Christlike attitude and actions that Paul calls the Philippians to in 2:1–8. Timothy exemplifies concern and selflessness (vv. 20–21). Both Timothy and Epaphroditus have "served" Paul in his need (vv. 22, 25). Epaphroditus is concerned for the Philippians; even selflessly concerned for their concern for him (v. 26). A supreme mark of Christlikeness, he was willing to lay down his life for the Philippians, for Paul, and for the gospel mission (v. 30). Paul never explicitly says that the Philippians should follow the examples of Timothy and Epaphroditus—he doesn't need to; it is clearly implied. While Christ is the perfect example (and the only saving sacrifice), God is good to give us imperfect but important examples of Christlikeness to watch and imitate. Paul will make this point more explicitly later in this letter (3:17; 4:9).

Whole-Bible Connections

THE MISSION. With all of the updates and personal commendations of 2:19–30, it might be easy to forget the most basic point behind all these comings and goings: the mission. That's why Paul is imprisoned and awaiting trial. That's why the Philippians sent support to Paul through Epaphroditus. It was the "work of Christ" for which he was "risking his life" (v. 30). For the sake of the mission, too, Timothy must stay with Paul for the time being (likely for Paul's defense); but he will return to Philippi as soon as possible to check up on the church (v. 19). His concern for their welfare is part of seeking the "interests ... of Jesus Christ" (v. 21). Sacrifice. Concern. Going. Serving. Risking. All for the sake of Christ and his mission. We shouldn't read 2:19–30 without remembering the gospel-priority in which Paul exulted in 1:12–18. And we shouldn't read 2:19–30 without remembering themes like the hope of global praise in Psalm 117 or the great commission in Matthew 28:18–20.

CARING FOR THE BODY. The Philippians' care and concern for Paul, and Timothy and Epaphroditus's care and concern for the Philippian believers, might bring to mind what Paul elsewhere writes about the nature of the church. In 1 Corinthians 12, for instance, he explains that the church is like a human body—one entity, but different parts doing different things for the common good. Some parts are small; some functions seem insignificant; but whether large or small, visible or hidden, all parts are needed (see 1 Cor. 12:18–23). That is why "God has so composed the body" with "no division" in it—so that "the members may have the same *care* for one another. If one member suffers, all suffer together; if one member is honored, all rejoice together" (vv. 24–26). This picture is exemplified in the communion[1] of mutual care shown in Philippians 2:18–30.

► Theological Soundings

GOD'S SOVEREIGNTY. Twice when speaking of his plans, Paul uses the phrase "in the Lord." He hopes "in the Lord" to soon send Timothy to Philippi (v. 19); he trusts "in the Lord" that he will eventually come as well (v. 24). Is Paul just tacking on superfluous spiritual language here? Far from it! Paul is echoing what James taught regarding the sin of making plans without acknowledging that God's sovereignty alone is decisive (James 4:13–16). James insists, "you ought to say, 'If the Lord wills, we will live and do this or that'" (v. 15). With different language, Paul is modeling this very thing. His plans are "in the Lord"—in his hands, up to him, subject to him. As Proverbs teaches, "man plans his way, but the LORD establishes his steps" (16:9). Epaphroditus knew this as well; he was "near to death" but "*God* had mercy on him" (Phil. 2:27). Our travel plans, our living and dying, and everything else, fall under God's providence[2] (see Acts 17:25–28). This reality not only needs to be believed and gladly embraced by Christians, but it also needs to be regularly *verbalized*, as both Paul and James show us.

► Personal Implications

Take time to reflect on the implications of Philippians 2:19–30 for your own life today. Consider what you have learned that might lead you to praise God, repent of sin, and trust in his gracious promises. Make notes below on the personal implications for your walk with the Lord of the (1) *Gospel Glimpses*, (2) *Whole-Bible Connections*, (3) *Theological Soundings*, and (4) this passage as a whole.

1. Gospel Glimpses

2. Whole-Bible Connections

3. Theological Soundings

4. Philippians 2:19–30

> ## As You Finish This Unit . . .

Take a moment now to ask for the Lord's blessing and help as you continue in this study of Philippians. And take a moment also to look back through this unit of study, to reflect on a few key things that the Lord may be teaching you—and perhaps to highlight and underline these things to review again in the future.

Definitions

[1] **Communion** – The fellowship and unity all believers share as a result of the work of the Holy Spirit in their hearts. Such communion among believers can be expressed in various ways, including worshiping God together, sharing possessions and resources, and partaking of the Lord's Supper, which has also come to be referred to as Communion.

[2] **Providence** – God's good, wise, and sovereign guidance and control of all things, by which he supplies all our needs and accomplishes his holy will.

Week 8: Rejoicing in the True and Only Gospel

Philippians 3:1–11

The Place of the Passage

Some have suggested that 3:1ff. seems like a strangely abrupt transition. But there are repeated themes and words in these verses that prove to be an orderly flow of thought from chapters 2–3. Having called the Philippians to hold fast to the "word of life" and to "rejoice" in mutual sacrifice for the gospel (2:16–18), and having shown Timothy and Epaphroditus to be Christlike models (2:19–30), Paul now further expounds upon that "word of life," contrasting false teaching with his own conversion and present confession (3:1–11).

The Big Picture

The Philippians are to follow Paul in rejoicing in the Lord by resisting false teachers who trust in the flesh, and glorying instead in Christ alone as their complete righteousness.

Reflection and Discussion

Read through Philippians 3:1–11, which will be the focus of this week's study. Following this, review the questions below concerning this section of the book of Philippians and write your responses. (For further background, see the *ESV Study Bible*, page 2285 or visit esv.org.)

Though 3:1 roughly marks the middle of the letter, Paul begins this section with "Finally . . ." The Greek word, however, might better be translated "So then"—which may suggest that Paul is picking up an earlier point. With the rest of 3:1 in mind, what theme/verses from chapter 2 might Paul be returning to?

What might be the connection between the command to "rejoice in the Lord" in 3:1 and what follows in verses 2–11?

Paul introduces this section in verse 1 by acknowledging that the things that follow are "the same things" he has told his readers before. To repeat them is "no trouble" for him, and it is "safe" for them. But why is it worth repeating what they've already heard?

In biblical times, Jews often referred to Gentiles as dogs (implying they were wild, impure, and outside). In verse 2 Paul warns of false teachers who require circumcision ("Judaizers[1]"), and he calls *them* "dogs." Why? What is he suggesting here?

Paul attests that because of Christ he has "suffered the loss of all things" (v. 8). Imagining the respectability, familiarity, and comfort of his former life as a religious leader, what might Paul have lost in embracing Christ? How does 2 Corinthians 11:23–29 further highlight this cost?

When Paul writes of what he used to consider "gain" (v. 7), what does he have in mind? Is he thinking in terms of *spiritual* gain or of the practical benefits (the "creaturely comforts") of his former way of life? Explain why.

Verse 9 uses the word "righteousness" in two different ways. One is *so-called* righteousness and the other is *true* righteousness. Describe the difference.

The gospel is infinitely glorious, rich, and expansive, but here Paul condenses the gospel message to a few short lines, making clear what it is and is not. Do the same in your own words. Imagine a friend asked you what he or she must do in order to be made right with God; what would you say?

What did Paul mean when he wrote of his longing to know "the power of his resurrection" (v. 10)?

When Paul writes that he longs to "share" Christ's "sufferings" (v. 10), he is striking a familiar note but in a new way. He has spoken numerous times about *partnership, partaking, participation, sharing,* etc. (e.g., 1:5, 7; 2:1; 4:14–15). The Philippians *share* in Paul's ministry and suffering (1:29–30). Now, Paul similarly seeks to *share* Christ's suffering. Explain the relationship between sharing the missionary sacrifice of others and sharing in the sufferings of Christ.

Compare these four phrases: "to know him," to know "the power of his resurrection," to "share in his sufferings," and "becoming like him in his death" (v. 10). Do you sense any tension or see any surprises between any of them? Explain.

Read through the following three sections on *Gospel Glimpses, Whole-Bible Connections*, and *Theological Soundings*. Then take time to consider the *Personal Implications* these sections may have for you.

Gospel Glimpses

NO RIGHTEOUSNESS/ALL RIGHTEOUSNESS. If anyone had reason to be confident in himself—in religious heritage, zeal, discipline, moral scruples, etc., it was Paul. He wasn't perfect, but compared with others, he was "blameless" (Phil. 3:6). Humanly speaking, he had attained all of the "righteousness" one could. But by God's intervening grace, Paul was shown that the only hope for being made right with God is to abandon any and all confidence in his own goodness and good works. His "achievements" achieved nothing. Actually, even worse, they were "loss," even "rubbish" (vv. 7–8). All self-trust must be renounced (such is repentance). Only then is one ready to see Jesus' life and death not as a "loss" but as a "gain." True righteousness "comes through faith in Christ"; it "depends on faith" (v. 9). Faith itself doesn't save, nor does trust in faith. Faith is looking outside of self to trust in "Christ, the righteousness of God" for us.

REPEATING THE GOSPEL. After reiterating his call to "rejoice in the Lord," Paul further introduces this section of Philippians with this: "To write the same things to you is no trouble to me and is safe for you" (v. 1). The "same things" that Paul goes on to write about in verses 2–9 are the truths of the gospel—warning of its distortion (v. 2) and explaining its essence through his own conversion (vv. 4–9). He had taught them these things before, but rehearsing them again is "safe." In fact, regardless of the conditions or times, repeating the gospel is *essential* for the church's fidelity and devotion. The gospel is "of first importance" (1 Cor. 15:3) and must be repeated, expounded, re-apprehended, and applied again and again.

KNOWING CHRIST. Philippians 3:1–11 is intensely personal, not only because Paul opens up his own life but also because of the way that he speaks of Christ. Salvation is desirable, of course, because sinners need forgiveness and the alternative is eternal condemnation; but it is ultimately desirable "because of the surpassing worth of *knowing* Christ Jesus" (v. 8). Christ is not merely the means to gain mercy, but mercy is the means by which we "gain Christ" (v. 8). Salvation is a Person.

Whole-Bible Connections

THE LAW VERSUS FAITH.[2] Paul's words—as well as his life—elucidate two different, opposing religious models. One model rests its confidence in the law and the flesh; the other rests in Christ's righteousness as a gift through faith. This raises the question of how Paul can seem to speak disparagingly about the law, since it was given by God who commanded his people to obey it. Indeed, Paul elsewhere attests that "the law is holy, and the commandment is holy and righteous and good" (Rom. 7:12). But how one *uses* the law makes all the difference in the world. God intended the Mosaic law primarily as a preparation for the righteousness that would come through the Messiah (see Gal. 3:23–25). But, like many Jews in his day, Paul had grown up trusting "a righteousness of [his] own that comes from the law" (Phil. 3:9). Obedience to the law was the primary basis for a right standing with God. He later came to see that "Christ is the end of the law for righteousness for everyone who believes" (Rom. 10:3). But many in his day, even some professing Christians, hadn't rightly understood this. Some mingled Christ and this distorted view of the law. They imposed the legal demands of the law on others, especially Gentiles, who, in their reckoning, needed to be circumcised[3] and to keep the law. But such barking "dogs" (Phil. 3:2) should be ignored, Paul insists. Those who have the *true* circumcision "worship by the Spirit, . . . and glory in Christ . . . and put no confidence in the flesh" (v. 3).

Theological Soundings

RESURRECTION FROM THE DEAD.[4] Paul's highest hope and longing was in "the resurrection from the dead" (v. 11). This is a culminating event in God's plan, when the bodies of living and dead believers will rise and be made new like Christ's post-resurrection body (1 Cor. 15:35–55). They will dwell in a new heaven and new earth without corruption, death, sin, conflict, curse, or threat (Rev. 21:1–5). They will be "glorified"[5] in that they will be like Jesus and will "see him as he is" (1 John 3:2). God will forever dwell with his people, fulfilling all his grand promises.

> ## Personal Implications

Take time to reflect on the implications of Philippians 3:1–11 for your own life today. Consider what you have learned that might lead you to praise God, repent of sin, and trust in his gracious promises. Make notes below on the personal implications for your walk with the Lord of the (1) *Gospel Glimpses*, (2) *Whole-Bible Connections*, (3) *Theological Soundings*, and (4) this passage as a whole.

1. Gospel Glimpses

2. Whole-Bible Connections

3. Theological Soundings

4. Philippians 3:1–11

> ## As You Finish This Unit . . .

Take a moment now to ask for the Lord's blessing and help as you continue in this study of Philippians. And take a moment also to look back through this unit of study, to reflect on a few key things that the Lord may be teaching you—and perhaps to highlight and underline these things to review again in the future.

Definitions

[1] **Judaizers** – Though this term is never actually used in the Bible, it refers to those in the early church who sought to compel Gentile believers to adhere to Jewish ceremonial requirements, such as circumcision, as a necessary part of salvation.

[2] **Faith** – Trust in or reliance upon something or someone despite a lack of concrete proof. Salvation, which is purely a work of God's grace, can be received only through faith (Rom. 5:2; Eph. 2:8–9). The writer of Hebrews calls on believers to emulate those who lived godly lives by faith (Hebrews 11).

[3] **Circumcision** – The ritual practice of removing the foreskin of an individual, which was commanded for all male Israelites in OT times as a sign of participation in the covenant God established with Abraham (Gen. 17:9–14).

[4] **Resurrection** – The impartation of new, eternal life to a dead person at the end of time (or in the case of Jesus, on the third day after his death). This new life is not a mere resuscitation of the body (as in the case of Lazarus; John 11:1–44) but a transformation of the body to an eternal state (1 Cor. 15:35–58). Both the righteous and the wicked will be resurrected, the former to eternal life and the latter to judgment (John 5:29).

[5] **Glorification** – The work of God in believers to bring them to the ultimate and perfect stage of salvation—Christlikeness—following his justification and sanctification of them (Rom. 8:29–30). Glorification includes believers receiving imperishable resurrection bodies at Christ's return (1 Cor. 15:42–43).

Week 9: Pressing Forward in Pursuit of Christ

Philippians 3:12–21

The Place of the Passage

Paul warned the Philippians about false teachers in 3:2. Their distortion of the gospel led him to use his own life as illustrative of a wrong (vv. 4–6) and a right (vv. 7–9) understanding of the gospel. The true gospel looks to Christ alone for righteousness, but then pursues further intimacy and identification with him (vv. 10–11). Now clarifying that the Christian life is imperfect and in process, Paul appeals to the Philippians to follow his example and not that of false teachers (vv. 18–19).

The Big Picture

The Christian life is neither one of perfection nor of passivity, but a progressive pursuit of Christ and his likeness as we await his return and the consummation of all things.

> ## Reflection and Discussion

Read through Philippians 3:12–21, which will be the focus of this week's study. Following this, review the questions below concerning this section of the book of Philippians and write your responses. (For further background, see the *ESV Study Bible*, page 2286 or visit esv.org.)

Last week's passage ended on a high, exultant note (vv. 1–11) while this week's begins in a more tempered tone. How might verses 12–14 be a clarification of verses 1–11? Looking through the rest of the passage (vv. 15–21), do you see any other reason why Paul writes about his imperfect pursuit of Christ in verses 12–13?

Verse 12 provides three motivating factors in Paul's pursuit of Christ. Why does Paul "press on," according to this verse?

Paul writes that his aim in pressing on is "to make it my own" (v. 12). What does he mean by this phrase? How does it relate to the next phrase, "because Christ Jesus has made me his own"?

What language does Paul use in verses 12–14 to describe his approach to the Christian life? What imagery is he conveying? What does it say about the nature of Christian growth?

What "lies behind" that Paul resolves to "forget" (v. 13)? (Hint: don't limit your consideration to negative things of the past.)

Paul attests that he is constantly "straining forward to what *lies ahead*," "toward the *goal*," which is "the *prize* of the *upward call*" (vv. 13–14). What is he referring to here? Is this a theme found elsewhere in Philippians 3?

When Paul speaks to "those . . . who are *mature*" in verse 15, he uses the same Greek word as in verse 12: "Not that I . . . am already *perfect*." He is *not* perfect, but then he addresses those who *are* perfect. How do we reconcile these two things? Is Paul speaking with "tongue-in-cheek" in verse 15? Explain.

In verses 15–16 Paul addresses those who "think otherwise"—i.e., other than his view of the Christian life in verses 12–14. What does he say to them? What doctrinal and pastoral assumptions stand behind Paul's approach?

Remarkably, after fully acknowledging his imperfection (vv. 12–13), Paul calls the Philippians to "join in imitating me" (v. 17). This is a call not infrequently issued by Paul (Phil. 4:9; 1 Cor. 11:1; 2 Thess. 3:8–9; 1 Tim. 4:12, 15–16), so why do many of us find it remarkable? Why are we often leery of watching and imitating imperfect Christians, let alone serving as models ourselves?

Paul warns of false teachers in 3:2 and 3:18–19. Do you think that these two passages refer to the same group? Why or why not? (For help, see the notes on pp. 2285–2286 of the ESV Study Bible.)

Paul uses five powerfully descriptive phrases for the false teachers in verses 18–19. What are they? In what ways might these phrases be contrasts of previous themes in Philippians?

Paul ends this section by writing of our heavenly "citizenship" (vv. 2–21). We are already *now* citizens of heaven, and yet we *"await* a Savior" and the transformation of our bodies. How should we think of our heavenly citizenship as a *now-and-not-yet* reality?

Read through the following three sections on *Gospel Glimpses, Whole-Bible Connections,* **and** *Theological Soundings.* **Then take time to consider the** *Personal Implications* **these sections may have for you.**

Gospel Glimpses

JESUS HAS MADE ME HIS OWN. Quite similar to Philippians 2:12–13 ("work out your own salvation . . . *for* it is God who works in you") Paul writes in 3:12–13, "I press on to make it my own, *because* Christ Jesus has made me his own." Both passages stress the complementary truths of human responsibility and divine sovereignty. What is unique about 3:12–13, however, is the personal, even intimate, tone: "Jesus has made me his own." Whether in initial grace or in ongoing sanctification, the reality is not simply that God works (or draws, or changes, or grows, or purifies—all good and important!), but that Jesus is making us his own. He is powerfully at work in us *because* he has taken us as his own. This should daily energize us, as it did Paul, to "press on to make it my own," even "straining forward" to Christ and Christlikeness (Phil. 3:12–14).

FROM LOWLINESS TO GLORY. Paul ends this chapter by rejoicing that when Jesus returns he "will transform our lowly body to be like his glorious body" (v. 21). The path from lowliness to glory is a well-trodden one by this point in Philippians. The supreme example is that of Christ in his incarnation and crucifixion,[1] leading to his resurrection and exaltation (2:5–11). Similarly, Paul's life being "poured out as a drink offering" (in execution) is something to "rejoice" in since it will demonstrate, at the "day of Christ," that he "did not run in vain" (vv. 16–17). Epaphroditus, too, was "near to death" (v. 27) because of his service to Paul on the Philippians' behalf. God rescued him from life-threatening sickness; thus, the church should "honor" him (v. 29). Paul, again in chapter 3, recounts his great "loss" for the sake of Christ (vv. 4–8)—a passage that ends with his expectation and longing to "attain the resurrection from the dead" (v. 11). So, too, 3:21 treks that path between present lowliness ("our lowly body") and future glory ("transform our lowly body to be like his glorious body"). All put together, it is clear that Paul is making an important point!

Whole-Bible Connections

ALL THINGS SUBJECTED TO JESUS. Paul speaks of "the power that enables" Christ "to subject all things to himself" (v. 21). He has already made the point that, because of who Christ is and because of his obedient death, he was raised and is now "highly exalted" (2:5–11). His power and authority are supreme and universal. In that sense, all things have *already* been subjected to him (1 Cor. 15:28; 1 Pet. 3:22). But experience as well as God's Word tells us that much of the world still does not bow before or confess Christ. Hebrews explains this: the Father has put "everything in subjection to him" and "left nothing outside his control"; but "at present, we do not yet see everything in subjection to him" (Heb. 2:8). When the King returns a second time, his rule, authority, and power will be universally and unavoidably manifest (Phil. 2:1–11). The power that will one day abolish all earthly authority, enemies, even Satan, and death itself, is *the same power* that will "transform our lowly body to be like his glorious body." He will do it "by the power that enables him even to subject all things to himself" (v. 21).

Theological Soundings

INDWELLING SIN. When Paul acknowledges his spiritual imperfection in Philippians 3:12–14, he is assuming a theological category that is fundamental to the Christian life. The absence of perfection assumes the presence of sin. While sin's dominion has been crushed by God's regenerating grace (Rom. 6:1–14), and his law has been written on the heart, creating new desires (Jer. 31:33), there is a principle of remaining indwelling sin—what Paul often calls "the flesh"[2] (Rom. 13:14; Gal. 5:16–23; Col. 2:23). Sin has been dealt a deathblow in regeneration, but it dies a slow death. In many ways, it is still quite active. The passions of the flesh "wage war against your soul" (1 Pet. 2:11). This is a slow and lifelong war. Thus, hard work is assumed in Paul's language of "pressing on" and "straining forward." But progress is also assumed. The race is run in steps—often small (and at times backward!), but we pray and strive for "progress" (Phil. 1:25). Such growth isn't gained through performance of the law (3:2) but in knowing and seeking Christ (3:1–14; see also 2 Cor. 3:18).

HEAVEN. Philippians 3:20 says that "our citizenship is in heaven." What is heaven? At the consummation of all things there will be a completely reconstructed creation, a new heaven and a new earth (Rev. 21–22). However, heaven is not just a future reality and place. Nor is it simply the dwelling of those who die before Christ's return. Heaven is also a present, invisible reality for the saints living on earth. Every Christian is already "blessed . . . with every spiritual blessing in the heavenly places" (Eph. 1:3). Raised up with Christ in regeneration, we are mysteriously but really "seated . . . with him in the heavenly places" (Eph. 2:6). So when Paul writes "our citizenship is in heaven" (Phil. 3:20), he is not only encouraging us to think about where we *will go*, but also about where we *are now*. It is a concept as majestic as it is mysterious. We "see" this realm now only with the eyes of faith (2 Cor. 4:18). We must "set our minds" on it (Col. 3:2) and long for the day when "heaven" will not only become visible but will overtake and transform everything.

> ### Personal Implications

Take time to reflect on the implications of Philippians 3:12–21 for your own life today. Consider what you have learned that might lead you to praise God, repent of sin, and trust in his gracious promises. Make notes below on the personal implications for your walk with the Lord of the (1) *Gospel Glimpses*, (2) *Whole-Bible Connections*, (3) *Theological Soundings*, and (4) this passage as a whole.

1. Gospel Glimpses

2. Whole-Bible Connections

3. Theological Soundings

4. Philippians 3:12–21

As You Finish This Unit . . .

Take a moment now to ask for the Lord's blessing and help as you continue in this study of Philippians. And take a moment also to look back through this unit of study, to reflect on a few key things that the Lord may be teaching you—and perhaps to highlight and underline these things to review again in the future.

Definitions

[1] **Crucifixion** – A means of execution in which the person was fastened, by ropes or nails, to a crossbeam that was then raised and attached to a vertical beam, forming a cross (the root meaning of "crucifixion"). The process was designed to maximize pain and humiliation, and to serve as a deterrent for other potential offenders. Jesus suffered this form of execution (Matt. 27:32–56), not for any offense he had committed (Heb. 4:15) but as the atoning sacrifice for all who would believe in him (John 3:16).

[2] **Flesh** – Depending on the immediate context, either skin (Lev. 4:11), a living being (Gen. 6:13), or sinful human nature (Rom. 8:3).

Week 10: Fighting for Peace, Joy, Trust, and Right Thinking

Philippians 4:1–9

The Place of the Passage

By 4:1 Paul begins to wrap up his letter to the Philippians. He confronts one specific case of disunity in the church, providing them (and us) concrete directives for dealing with conflict (vv. 2–3). He then turns to a series of pithy commands (vv. 4–9), which in many ways summarize and materialize several themes and ideals from earlier in the epistle.

The Big Picture

The Philippians are to stand firm by pursuing peace, joy, gentleness, trust, prayer, and right thinking—matters that Paul has taught and modeled for them.

> ## Reflection and Discussion

Read through Philippians 4:1–9, which will be the focus of this week's study. Following this, review the questions below concerning this section of the book of Philippians and write your responses. (For further background, see the *ESV Study Bible*, pages 2286–2287 or visit esv.org.)

Verse 1 is a transitional sentence in that it looks back to what came before and forward to what's ahead. Which word in verse 1 points us backward? Which word points us forward? Also, how does Paul's call to "stand firm" (4:1) relate thematically to what came before (3:17–21) and what comes after (4:2–9)?

Looking through the whole of this section (vv. 1–9), which phrases can be classified as *command/exhortation*? Which phrases can be classified as *promise/basis*?

Paul addresses the church with six different affectionate terms in verse 1. Note them. Why do you think Paul stresses this so? Do you see any other warm, personal terms in verses 2–3?

We don't know the nature or details of the disagreement between the two ladies Paul addresses in verses 2–3, but his plea to "agree in the Lord" should remind us that unity (or a lack thereof) has been no small concern in Philippians. In fact, the same Greek phrase is used in 4:2 ("agree") and 2:2 ("the same mind"). What other verses in Philippians 1–3 have touched on the theme of unity?

Paul specifies the kind of joy he is calling the church to: it is "in the Lord" (v. 4). What does it mean to rejoice "in the Lord"?

In verse 5 Paul calls the Philippians to "reasonableness" (or gentleness) followed by a brief comment: "The Lord is at hand" (or near). What does Paul mean by this? What does the Lord's nearness have to do with the pursuit of gentleness?

Verse 6 issues one negative command (what not to do) and one positive command (what to do). What are they, and how do they relate to each other?

In your own words, what do circumstances have to do with joy, worry, and prayer?

In verse 6, Paul uses multiple words for prayer. What does each mean? How does each relate to resisting anxiety?

In verse 8, Paul provides eight parameters for our thinking. How might these serve as (1) a filter for what not to think, and (2) a prescription for what to pro-actively think (meditate[1]) upon?

In what practical ways might you proactively "think about" things that are true, honorable, just, etc. (v. 8)?

This section draws to a close with Paul reiterating his call to follow his example and teaching (v. 9). They are to "practice these things." Explain the significance of that word, "practice."

How might each of the commands in verses 4–9 be relevant to Paul's concern for unity in verses 2–3 and elsewhere?

Read through the following three sections on *Gospel Glimpses, Whole-Bible Connections*, and *Theological Soundings*. Then take time to consider the *Personal Implications* these sections may have for you.

Gospel Glimpses

IN THE LORD. In a short span Paul uses the phrase "in the Lord" three times. The church is to "stand firm . . . in the Lord" (v. 1), Euodia and Syntyche are to "agree in the Lord" (v. 2), and all are to "rejoice in the Lord" (v. 4). A few verses later, he writes similarly of hearts and minds being guarded "in Christ Jesus" (v. 7). Paul is a big fan of these "in" phrases: in him, in Christ, in the Lord, etc. With these "in" phrases Paul is alluding to the doctrine of the believer's "union with Christ." This union begins with being "found *in him,* not having a righteousness of my own . . . but that which comes through faith in Christ" (3:9). It is "in Christ" that we also receive all of God's saving promises and benefits (see 2:1, 5). Thus, "we glory in Christ Jesus" (3:3). What an important preposition!

FORGIVENESS AND RECONCILIATION. Because every believer is "in Christ," believers are in Christ together. Communion with Christ includes communion with others in the body of Christ (the church). Of course, this doesn't mean that there aren't disagreements or conflicts between Christians—even mature and experienced Christians; Euodia and Syntyche had "labored side by side" with Paul (v. 3), and yet their disagreement rose to such a level that news of it reached Rome. It troubled Paul enough that he addressed them by name in a public letter to the whole church. He pleads with them to "agree in the Lord" (v. 2). In essence he is saying, Ladies, recognize what you share; recognize your identity; recognize the saving benefits in Christ (2:1–2); and recognize them in each other. Paul isn't naive; he isn't suggesting that agreement can be reached by sweeping conflict under the rug. Concerns will have to be discussed, confession eventually made, forgiveness granted. But the relationships themselves are often complicated. Thus, Paul calls on a "true companion"—unknown to us but obviously known to Paul and the Philippians—to "help these women" get along (v. 3). This is simply the church exchanging self-interests for the "interests of others" (2:4), and working out salvation with one another (2:12). It is a corporate enterprise.

Whole-Bible Connections

PEACE. The concept of peace is fundamental to Philippians 4. Not only is the word used twice ("peace of God," v. 7; "God of peace," v. 9) but Paul also alludes to peace with other words. Euodia and Syntyche need to pursue peace (v. 2). A gentle spirit ("reasonableness"; v. 5) is one that is inwardly and outwardly at peace. Anxiety is the absence of inner peace. Prayer is the antidote to anxiety and the path to God's supernatural peace (vv. 6–7). Peace is also a theme significant to the whole Bible. In many ways God's plan can be charted through this lens: peace created in the garden, lost in the fall, and restored progressively by God. God's plan to restore peace is first seen in the promises and shadows of the Old Testament, but ultimately through the "Prince of Peace" (Isa. 9:6), Jesus, in the New Testament. In his coming, dying, and rising, and his Spirit's drawing, the peace of Christ penetrates lives, permeates relationships, and comforts hearts. The Prince of Peace will come again to bring final judgment on the world and final salvation to his own, thereby bringing all his promises for peace to their fulfillment.

THE BOOK OF LIFE. Paul refers to his ministry partners as people "whose names are in the book of life" (v. 3). This "book of life" is mentioned several times in the book of Revelation in connection with the final judgment (Rev. 3:5; 13:8; 17:8; 20:12, 15; 21:27). Moses spoke similarly when he asked God to either forgive the Israelites or "blot me out of your book that you have written" (Ex. 32:32). So too David when he lamented God's enemies: "Let them be blotted out of the book of the living; let them not be enrolled among the righteous" (Ps. 69:28). The imagery should be obvious. This book is the roll of God's "elect."

It divides all humanity. Those not in this book will face terrible, eternal demise (see Rev. 20:15). But those written in it by God's sovereign grace can rejoice even now. As Jesus told his disciples upon their return from a successful mission, "do not rejoice ... that the spirits are subject to you, but rejoice that your names are written in heaven" (Luke 10:20).

Theological Soundings

OMNIPRESENCE. When Paul writes the pithy words, "The Lord is at hand" (Phil. 4:5), he may have in mind the nearness of the Lord's return. This is certainly something Paul has referred to before in Philippians (1:10; 3:11, 21), and the ever-nearness of the second coming is something he spoke of elsewhere (1 Thess. 5:1). More likely, however, in Philippians 4:5 Paul has in mind the *spatial* nearness, not the *temporal* nearness of the Lord. Theologians call this God's "omnipresence." God is everywhere; he sees and knows all. Of course, this reality has significant implications and massive motivating power (as is Paul's intent in citing it in 4:5). Nothing is hidden from God's eyes (Jer. 16:17). This is an awe-filling reality. And yet God's omnipresence need not conjure up only feelings of fear and threat; it is enormously comforting for those who also know of the Lord's goodness and care (see Ps. 139:1–6).

SOVEREIGNTY. Paul sees the Christian's battle against anxiety as one fought by praying (Phil. 4:6). Such an equation pivots on the sovereignty of God. We pray because he is sovereign and we are not. We lack the power to alter most difficult circumstances; we lack the wisdom to know what is best; and we lack the perspective to know best in the grand scheme of God's plan. Whether explicitly spoken as such or not, anxiety signals discontentment with God's plan, or lack of confidence in it. Fretting implies that God doesn't see, doesn't care, or can't change things. The anxious heart turns inward, rehashing problems with *self*—almost as a form of self-prayer! But in *true* prayer, burdens are brought to the One who is wise and good, and he works accordingly. And he also supernaturally comforts and guards restless hearts (v. 7).

Personal Implications

Take time to reflect on the implications of Philippians 4:1–9 for your own life today. Consider what you have learned that might lead you to praise God, repent of sin, and trust in his gracious promises. Make notes below on the personal implications for your walk with the Lord of the (1) *Gospel Glimpses*, (2) *Whole-Bible Connections*, (3) *Theological Soundings*, and (4) this passage as a whole.

1. Gospel Glimpses

2. Whole-Bible Connections

3. Theological Soundings

4. Philippians 4:1–9

As You Finish This Unit . . .

Take a moment now to ask for the Lord's blessing and help as you continue in this study of Philippians. And take a moment also to look back through this unit of study, to reflect on a few key things that the Lord may be teaching you—and perhaps to highlight and underline these things to review again in the future.

Definitions

[1] **Meditation** – Contemplation on something, such as the attributes of God, with focused attention (see Ps. 1:2). Biblical meditation stands in contrast to many forms of Eastern meditation, which seek to empty the mind of rational thought.

Week 11: Provision, Thankfulness, and Contentment

Philippians 4:10–23

The Place of the Passage

After a series of summary exhortations (Phil. 4:1–9), and before his final greetings (vv. 22–23), Paul acknowledges with thanks the Philippian church's financial support, brought by Epaphroditus (vv. 10–21). This topic occurs elsewhere in the epistle (1:3–5; 2:25–30), making it a major theme and a primary reason for Paul's writing to the Philippians.

The Big Picture

Paul warmly thanks the Philippians for once again supporting his mission, but he also takes the opportunity to explain that he has learned to be content, with little or much.

> ## Reflection and Discussion

Read through Philippians 4:10–23, which will be the focus of this week's study. Following this, review the questions below concerning this section of the book of Philippians and write your responses. (For further background, see the *ESV Study Bible*, page 2287 or visit esv.org.)

Philippians 4 provides further insight into Paul's long history with this church. He alludes to several previous occasions where they supported his work (vv. 15–16). Now read 2 Corinthians 8:1–4, where Paul certainly has the Philippians in mind when he commends the giving of the "churches of Macedonia" (Philippi was a city in the region of Macedonia). How do these details further shed light on the warm, affectionate tone of Philippians (e.g., 1:3–8; 4:1)?

Looking back through the whole of Philippians 4, which verses and words speak to the *partnership* in the gospel that the Philippians shared with Paul? How should this theme factor into our understanding of the overall purposes and emphases of the letter?

In the middle of acknowledging the Philippians' support, Paul inserts a parenthetical comment about his contentment (vv. 11–13). Why do you think he did this? Are there potential misunderstandings that he might have been trying to avoid?

Paul testifies, "I can do all things through him who strengthens me" (v. 13). What does he mean by "all things"? What "things"? God "strengthens" him for what? (Hint: don't forget the importance of context!)

How might the exhortations from the previous section (especially 4:4–8) relate to the theme of contentment in this section (especially 4:11–13, 19)?

Based on Paul's language in verses 11–18, what can be determined about the *extent* of the Philippians' recent gift to Paul?

Again, based on Paul's own words, how did he come to be so content (vv. 11–13)? We know that his testimony isn't sinful boasting, but *how* do we know that?

The ideas in verses 17–19 are also found in 2 Corinthians 9:5–15 in greater detail. Read both passages and compare. What themes and language do they share?

Paul uses Old Testament ceremonial worship language when referring to the Philippians' support (v. 18). What is Paul suggesting by this? Where else in Philippians have we seen this sort of language?

In verses 14–20 Paul mingles *thanks* to the Philippians and *praise* to God. He does the same in other letters. But why? What is Paul teaching us by this model? What is different about doing one without the other?

Read through the following three sections on *Gospel Glimpses, Whole-Bible Connections,* and *Theological Soundings.* Then take time to consider the *Personal Implications* these sections may have for you.

Gospel Glimpses

GIVEN MUCH, GIVING MUCH. Christians should, by their nature and their experience of grace, have a strong impulse to give to others—to those in need, to the church as a whole, to missionaries, etc. Having been given so much (in Christ), there is a desire to give much (for Christ). Paul makes this very clear in 2 Corinthians 8:1–9. Paul tells the (sometimes stingy) Corinthians about the exemplary generosity of the Macedonian churches. Despite their poverty, they gave "in a wealth of generosity" and with an "abundance of joy" (v. 3). They gave "of their own accord," even "begging" to be included in the relief of the more greatly impoverished saints in Jerusalem. Eventually Paul brings his appeal to a fine gospel-point. Giving like this proves that "love . . . is genuine. *For* you know the grace of our Lord Jesus Christ, that though he was rich, yet for your sake he became poor, so that you by his poverty might become rich" (vv. 8–9). So, having received greatly, give greatly—not as any kind of repayment for Christ's saving sacrifice, but with joy, as an "act of grace" (v. 7). Generosity should flow from the believer's "confession of the gospel" (9:13).

Whole-Bible Connections

CONCERN, SHARING, PARTNERSHIP. These words and others like them are scattered throughout Philippians 4—and, indeed, over the whole epistle. The Philippians' recent financial support was the primary impetus for Paul writing to them. He acknowledges their support multiple times before giving a more formal and thorough thanks in 4:10–20. As was suggested in our study of Philippians 2:19–30, so too here, it is possible to miss the forest for the trees in such a passage. The key words are *sharing, concern, need, partnership, giving* (the trees). But the *why* behind those words (the forest) is that the gospel must get to the Gentiles, especially those who have not heard (Rom. 15:20). That is why Paul is often in "need," why the Philippians have "concern," why "giving and receiving" is necessary. Whether in Paul's day or our own, missions are needed because God is intent to redeem a multitude from *every tribe, language, people,* and *nation* (Rev. 5:9).

A FRAGRANT OFFERING AND SACRIFICE. Paul describes the Philippians' gift as "a fragrant offering, a sacrifice acceptable and pleasing to God" (v. 18). This kind of ceremonial worship language is found throughout the Old Testament (e.g., Gen. 8:21; Ex. 29:18; Lev. 4:31). While such burnt offerings and sacrifices have been done away with in the coming of the true and final Sacrifice (see Heb. 8–10), Paul is making a quick and powerful analogy. The Philippians' financial support was an act of worship. It was sent *to Paul*, but in a very real sense it was also *to God*. It was "pleasing to God"—it *smelled* good to him. The Philippians, and we today, are called to be deliberate about this worshipful dimension to giving. (For more on giving, and particularly the differences between giving in the old and new covenant[1] eras, see the article "Stewardship" on pages 2559–2560 in the *ESV Study Bible*.)

Theological Soundings

ALL TO GOD'S GLORY. After reflecting on how the Philippians' gracious gift pleased the Lord (v. 18) and how God would supply all of their needs "according to his riches in glory in Christ Jesus" (v. 19), Paul explodes in a doxological[2] declaration: "To our God and Father be glory forever and ever. Amen" (v. 20). This is our "chief end," according to the Westminster Catechism, to "glorify God and enjoy him forever." This is also *God's* chief end, according to the Bible. His interest in his own glory is relentless and pervasive. Again and again, we are told that God did this or that thing "for his glory," "for his renown," "for his name's sake," even "for his fame." He is intent on revealing his glory to the whole world, especially his people, and to show that glory preeminently through his Son (Phil. 2:1–11). It is right and loving for God to pursue and promote his own glory like this, because he *is* glorious. He is "great . . . and greatly to be praised" (Ps. 145:3).

Personal Implications

Take time to reflect on the implications of Philippians 4:10–23 for your own life today. Consider what you have learned that might lead you to praise God, repent of sin, and trust in his gracious promises. Make notes below on the personal implications for your walk with the Lord of the (1) *Gospel Glimpses*, (2) *Whole-Bible Connections*, (3) *Theological Soundings*, and (4) this passage as a whole.

1. Gospel Glimpses

2. Whole-Bible Connections

3. Theological Soundings

4. Philippians 4:10–23

> ### As You Finish This Unit . . .

Take a moment now to ask for the Lord's blessing and help as you continue in this study of Philippians. And take a moment also to look back through this unit of study, to reflect on a few key things that the Lord may be teaching you—and perhaps to highlight and underline these things to review again in the future.

Definitions

[1] **Covenant** – A binding agreement between two parties, typically involving a formal statement of their relationship, a list of stipulations and obligations for both parties, a list of witnesses to the agreement, and a list of curses for unfaithfulness and blessings for faithfulness to the agreement. The OT is more properly understood as the old covenant, meaning the agreement established between God and his people prior to the coming of Jesus Christ and the establishing of the new covenant (NT).

[2] **Doxology** – Expression of praise to God. Often included at the end of NT letters. Modern church services often end with doxologies in the form of short hymns.

WEEK 12: SUMMARY AND CONCLUSION

We will conclude our study of Philippians by summarizing the big picture of God's message through Philippians as a whole. Then we will consider several questions in order to reflect on various *Gospel Glimpses, Whole-Bible Connections,* and *Theological Soundings* throughout the entire book.

The Big Picture of Philippians

On behalf of the concerned Philippians, Epaphroditus risked his life in getting support to Paul, who was imprisoned in Rome. Upon his arrival, Epaphroditus was also able to report on the state of the Philippian church to the concerned apostle. Thus, while Philippians is primarily a letter of thanks for financial support and an update on the *comings* and *goings* of key people, Paul also writes to confront and instruct in the areas most needed in Philippi at the time.

In chapter 1, Paul acknowledges the Philippians' concern for his imprisonment with affection and thanks, but he redirects their concerns and priorities. He explains that his imprisonment is really no problem at all, but has in fact been good for the spread of the gospel in Rome. His possible execution is no problem either, since death would enable him to be with Christ.

Paul also writes to confront a trend of disunity and selfishness in the body (1:27–2:18). In chapter 3, he warns about false teachers in the area, and reiterates the truth of the gospel to which the church must tightly hold. He also reminds them that the Christian life is a race to be run with endurance. In chapter 4, Paul highlights how perseverance and growth significantly involve the faculties of the inner man: the mind, the heart, feelings, and thoughts.

Perhaps some of the Philippian Christians had grown passive in their Christian life. Maybe some (or many) had grown soft, afraid of suffering, quick to complain, slow to reconcile, and/or gripped by worry. Perhaps some had taken their eyes off their heavenly home and had lost the powerfully motivating hope of Christ's return. Such matters are addressed in Philippians, not arbitrarily but most likely by necessity.

Nevertheless, whether he is thanking, confronting, or instructing the Philippians, Paul's pen drips with warmth and affection throughout the letter. Reminders of his love and care for them, and their long-standing partnership in the gospel, are ever present. He calls on them as a brother who is side by side with them in the faith, not commanding them with all the weight of his apostolic authority. Throughout, he calls on them to emulate the humble, sacrificial example of others: Paul himself, Epaphroditus, Timothy, and especially Jesus.

▶ Gospel Glimpses

We have seen that the gospel saturates Philippians. Paul gives a uniquely thorough and personal exposition of the gospel in chapter 3. While primarily intended as a model of humility, Paul's words on Christ's incarnation, servanthood, suffering, death, and exaltation in chapter 2 are a window into the basis of gospel hope. Throughout Philippians the gospel's implications are far-reaching: life-transforming, joy-giving, and saint-connecting. Thus, the spread of the gospel in the world is of utmost importance. The gospel is to be lived out and proclaimed; it is to be taken far and wide; and those who take it are to be supported.

Has this study of Philippians brought new clarity to your understanding of the gospel? How so?

Were there any particular passages or themes in Philippians that led you to have a fresh understanding and grasp of God's grace to us through Jesus?

Whole-Bible Connections

Philippians has numerous connections to the Old Testament promises, such as God's grace among the Gentiles, the coming of the suffering servant and exalted King, God dwelling with his people, the inevitable path from suffering to glory, and the consummation of all things.

How has this study of Philippians grown your understanding of the storyline of Bible?

What are some connections between Philippians and the Old Testament that you hadn't noticed before?

Have any passages or themes expanded your understanding of the redemption that Jesus provides, which he began at his first coming and will consummate at his return?

Theological Soundings

We have seen that Philippians is intensely personal and practical, but also richly doctrinal. Its doctrinal themes include: Christ's eternality, deity, incarnation, and dual natures; the return of Christ, the bodily resurrection, and the consummation of all things; justification and union with Christ; the nature of sanctification and perseverance; God's sovereignty, and its relationship to human responsibility in salvation and sanctification.

Has your theology shifted in any minor or major ways during the course of studying Philippians? How so?

How has your understanding of the nature and character of God been deepened throughout this study?

What unique contributions does Philippians make toward our understanding of who Jesus is and what he accomplished through his life, death, and resurrection?

What, specifically, does Philippians teach us about the human condition and our need of redemption?

Personal Implications

God wrote the book of Philippians to transform us. As you reflect on Philippians as a whole, what implications do you see for your life?

What implications for life flow from your reflections on the questions already asked in this week's study concerning Gospel Glimpses, Whole-Bible Connections, and Theological Soundings?

What have you learned in Philippians that might lead you to praise God, turn away from sin, or trust more firmly in his promises?

▶ As You Finish Studying Philippians . . .

We rejoice with you as you finish studying the book of Philippians! May this study become part of your Christian walk of faith, day by day and week by week throughout all your life. Now we would greatly encourage you to continue to study the Word of God on a week-by-week basis. To continue your study of the Bible, we would encourage you to consider other books in the *Knowing the Bible* series, and to visit www.knowingthebibleseries.org.

Lastly, take a moment again to look back through this book of Philippians, which you have studied during these recent weeks. Review again the notes that you have written, and the things that you have highlighted or underlined. Reflect again on the key themes that the Lord has been teaching you about himself and about his Word. May these things become a treasure for you throughout your life—which we pray will be true for you, in the name of the Father, and the Son, and the Holy Spirit. Amen.